KU-111-127

ROCK CLIMBS IN ARRAN

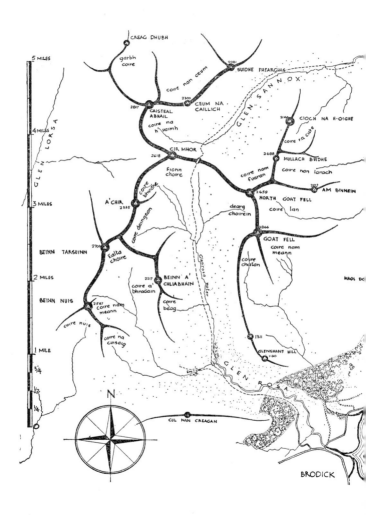

CREAG DHUBH

garbh
coire

5 MILES

coire nan ceum

2081
SUIDHE FHEARGHAS

2300
CEUM NA
CAILLICH

2817
CAISTEAL
ABHAIL

coire na
h'uaimh

GLEN SANNOX

4 MILES

2168
CIOCH NA H-OIGHE

coire na ciar

CIR MHOR
2618

2688
MULLACH BUIDHE

coire nam larach

Fionn
choire

coire nam
fuaran

2817
AM BINNEIN

coire
bhradie

A'CHIR
2335

dearg
choirein

2659
NORTH GOAT FELL

coire lan

coire daingean

2706
BEINN TARSUINN

Ealta
choire

2866
GOAT FELL

coire nam
meann

2217
BEINN A'
CHLIABHAIN

coire
chatan

coire a'
bhradain

2597
coire nam
meann

coire
beag

coire nuis

BEINN NUIS

Cioreas water

coire na
cuisaig

1311

GLENSHANT HILL
1130

3/4

1/2

1/4

N

CUL NAN CREAGAN

GLEN ROSA

BRODICK

KAOL DO

GLEN LORSA

ROCK CLIMBS

IN

ARRAN

BY

J. M. JOHNSTONE

PUBLISHED BY
THE SCOTTISH MOUNTAINEERING TRUST
369 HIGH STREET, EDINBURGH
1963

FIRST PUBLISHED . . . 1958
REPRINT, WITH APPENDIX, 1963

PRINTED IN GREAT BRITAIN BY
ROBERT CUNNINGHAM AND SONS LTD., ALVA

FOREWORD

DURING the preparation of this little guide I have been assisted by many friends, but it is not invidious, I think, to record my indebtedness to certain of them. Above all, I must mention W. C. Harrison (J.M.C.S.) who has drawn all the diagrams and endured many wet and miserable weekends in Arran these past summers on my behalf. I have also been fortunate in being able to draw upon the unrivalled experience of climbing in Arran of Miss Grace Hamilton and W. Wallace (J.M.C.S.). Lastly, I should like to pay tribute to the General Guide Books Editor for his help and advice throughout the period of compilation, which must have seemed to him inordinately long.

J. M. JOHNSTONE

November 1958.

CONTENTS

PART III

DIAGRAMS

INTRODUCTION

THE shapely peaks and well defined ridges of the Arran Hills, which one cannot fail to admire from the steamer as it approaches the island, are the remains of a dome of very coarse-crystalled granite. Shortly after it had welled up a large number of basalt dykes were thrust through the granitic mass and during cooling a widespread system of joints in three distinct planes developed. These events coupled with the continual action of the forces of denudation have produced a unique type of rock scenery. The three-dimensional joints are responsible for the cyclopean-block walls and the great over-lapping slabs and the principal gullies are the decayed remains of basalt dykes, hence their poor quality as rock climbs. From a rock climbing point of view the structure of the rock is on the whole disadvantageous. Holds are either generous or entirely lacking. To enjoy Arran climbing one must be prepared for abrupt transitions from delicate balance moves on a steep slab to strenuous jamming in a holdless chimney or crack. Undoubtedly the exceptional roughness of the rock assists such manoeuvres, giving one a feeling of painful security. In wet conditions however these adhesive properties are sometimes diminished by the presence of rock dust and lichen. Vibrams can thus be treacherous if not used with great care. A shortage of good belays is another direct consequence of the rock structure. Accordingly, it is advisable to allow 120 ft. of rope per man if possible. Piton belays can occasionally be useful but in general suitable fissures are not plentiful. A length of nylon line should be carried for constructing thread belays in places where full weight rope cannot be introduced.

9

ACCESS

British Railways operate steamer services *on weekdays only* to Brodick from Ardrossan in the summer (June-September) and from Fairlie during the remainder of the year.

ACCOMMODATION ETC.

There are a few hotels and numerous boarding houses at Brodick, Corrie and Sannox. To get a longer climbing day one should camp in Glen Rosa or Glen Sannox. The former is particularly rich in suitable sites and the Rosa Burn provides some delectable swimming pools.

Provisions are easily obtained at Brodick and Corrie. Outside the summer months, the early closing day is Wednesday. Climbing gear, camping equipment, maps and guide books are not on sale.

HISTORY

Arran was discovered as a climbing area by members of the S.M.C. in the 1890s and by the beginning of the twentieth century had been fully reconnoitred. Gullies and chimneys were the usual line of attack in those days so that, given the mediocre qualities of almost all Arran gullies, it was not surprising that, apart from the sensational ascent of the Nuis Chimney, no really first-class climbing emerged from this first wave of exploration. Forty years passed before the second or "open face" period of discovery got under way, the main stimulus being the direct ascent of the Rosa Pinnacle's South Ridge by J. F. Hamilton and D. Paterson in 1941. Before the end of World War II G. C. Curtis and G. H. Townend had carried out a thorough exploration of the island's rock climbing possibilities and the many good routes they pioneered are a monument to their diligence and enterprise.

THE CLIMBS

The layout of the guide is as follows:

      1. Routes in the Glen Rosa Basin.

      2. Routes in the Glen Sannox Basin.

      3. Routes situated outside 1 and 2.

The usual grading system (for Vibram soles) has been used and directions left/right apply when one faces the rock. Following continental fashion, the routes are numbered for ease of identification.

INDEX TO CLIMBS

13

PART I

GLEN ROSA BASIN

BEINN NUIS, 2597 feet

The most southerly of the granite peaks forms the dominating feature of the view as one walks up lower Glen Rosa. The eastern face containing all the rock climbs is clearly seen. Leave the main track where a water pipe bridges the Rosa Burn and follow the track branching left, which climbs up the southern hillside to a small barrage across the Garbh Allt, the turbulent tributary which joins the Rosa where the Glen turns abruptly north. Once across the burn, head ENE over gently rising moor into Coire a' Bhradain and thence to the subsidiary Coire nam Meann below the face. Five gullies or fissures split the precipice, the central one being the notorious Nuis Chimney.

1. ANVIL GULLY   120 feet   Moderate

Left of Gully 1 the SE ridge of the mountain forms a large cyclopean wall below which a grass rake slants up to the left. Anvil Gully lies below and parallel to this rake. There is some amusing caving but little climbing. Recommended for stormy weather only.

First ascent: G. C. Curtis, E. J. W. Morrison and M. H. J. Hawkins. April 1946.

2. GULLY 1   300 feet   Difficult

An unpleasant ill-defined route on loose rock. Not recommended.

First ascent: W. Inglis Clark and H. Raeburn. *Circa* 1897.

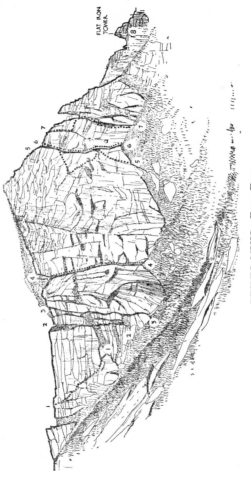

BEINN NUIS EAST FACE

1. Anvil Gully
2. Gully 1
3. Gully 2
4. The Chimney
5. Suckers Slabs
6. Gully 4
7. Gully 5 (Green and Boyd)
8. Flat Iron Tower

3. GULLY 2   300 feet   Difficult

Similar to Gully 1. About two thirds up, a right traverse can be made into Gully 3 above its difficulties. Not recommended.

First ascent: W. Inglis Clark and H. Raeburn. 1897.

4. GULLY 3 (The Chimney)   430 feet   Very Severe

The first ascent of this chimney by Baker, Puttrell and Oppenheimer in 1901 as chronicled in Volume 7 of the *S.M.C. Journal* involved several excursions on to the dangerous faces flanking the fissure and so made the enterprise so hazardous that the climb was not repeated, it is thought, until 1955. It was found then to be perfectly feasible and safe to keep in the chimney all the way. Possibly a rock fall since 1901 is the reason. A prolonged dry spell and a supply of blade type pitons are required before attempting this route. The foot of the chimney is marked by a prominent cone of turf which terminates in a repulsive scoop of decomposing granite.

(1) 70 feet. Scramble up to a small grass platform above which the scoop perceptibly steepens. There are holds for a few feet and then one is confronted with the slime-streaked, holdless chimney bed lying at a high angle between walls too far apart to straddle. This section was overcome by combined tactics on the first ascent (three or more persons required). Alternatively drive blade type pitons into the right-hand incipient crack and so with the use of rope slings or, better, "étriers" conquer the bulge. Great care is necessary for the pitons tend to come out. A further 20 feet up the mossy bed there is a good crack on the left wall for a belay (piton).

(2) 50 feet. Proceed back and foot (face right) until it

is possible to use the bed. Pass beneath jammed block and reach it by back and foot (face left). Good stance and belay.

(3) 90 feet. Use vertical back wall of the chimney followed by more back and foot work to reach a little platform. The next 30 feet are easier and then a group of chock stones is reached. There is a through route to a good belay.

(4) 40 feet. Steep grass and moss leads in 20 feet to a large overhanging block. Scale this and follow the narrow chimney (cluttered with aircraft wreckage) above to a large stance.

(5) 50 feet. The chimney suddenly widens and is divided by a rib of rock. Climb the deeply cut left branch to a jammed block. This pitch is very strenuous as the cleft admits the body sideways with little room for manoeuvre. Stout climbers may be tempted to use the right wall and succeeding slabs to a point level with the jammed block but the traverse (loose turf) is so hazardous that they should risk becoming permanently wedged in the cleft.

(6) 70 feet. Proceed back and foot (face right) until the chimney again narrows. Reach a tiny cave by good hidden handholds on right wall and exit by the right wall to open ground.

(7) 60 feet. Steep grass and a through route lead to the summit.

Apart from the last pitch (Easy) the route is continuously severe (Pitch (1) Very Severe).

First Direct ascent: W. C. Harrison and J. M. Johnstone (alternate leads). August 1955.

5. SUCKERS SLABS   500 feet   Very Severe

This dangerous climb is the only one so far made up the face of the Nuis precipice. G. C. Curtis, G. H. Townend and H. K. Moneypenny, who made the ascent on 27th June 1943 (in stockings), extricated themselves by a most hazardous traverse over unstable turf. *Vide S.M.C. Journal*, Vol. 23, No. 135.

An *unjustifiable* climb, hence no description is given.

6. GULLY 4   400 feet   Easy

Mainly a walk over grass and scree.
First ascent: S.M.C. party in 1895.

7. GULLY 5 (Green and Boyd)   300 feet   Difficult

A scrappy climb. There is a short chimney pitch near the start. Below cave near the top, traverse left into a 40 ft. chimney. From the finish, Messrs Green and Boyd "climbed obliquely up grass ledges and easy rocks, stepping off the face on to the very summit of the mountain".
First ascent: Messrs Green and Boyd. 1895.

8. FLAT-IRON TOWER   100 feet   Moderate

Just south of the Nuis—Tarsuinn Col there is a tor giving at least two short routes.
First ascent: unknown.

BEINN TARSUINN, 2706 feet

North of the Nuis—Tarsuinn Col there are several small cliffs falling into Coire a' Bhradain, and above its northern bay, known as Ealta Coire, an extensive mass of rock, the Meadow Face, rises steeply. There are also a few short climbs on the Coire Daingean slopes of the mountain.

9. FULL MEED CHIMNEY   200 feet   Very Difficult

This deeply cut chimney splits the large tower-like buttress north of the Nuis—Tarsuinn Col and the start

of the climb is most easily reached by descending the
gully south of the buttress. There are three pitches to
this "satisfying" route.

(1) 70 feet. Climb chimney to chock stones. (*Variation*: Ascend broken crack on face left of the chimney
to horizontal ledge of Pitch (2)).

(2) 50 feet. Move along ledge to the left and enter
narrow crack which will just admit the body. Wriggle
up and emerge on large block platform. Climb continuation of crack in right-angled corner above.

(3) 80 feet. Trend rightwards to the nose and thence
to the top.

First ascent: unknown.

Variation by J. S. Stewart and J. M. Johnstone (who
were ignorant of original route) in September 1952.

10. SWILDON'S GULLY   150 feet   Moderate

This boulder-filled cleft lies on the south-eastern side
of a large nameless tor between Full Meed Tower and
the summit. It was exotically named after a well-known
feature in the Mendips. The route tunnels through many
boulders and finishes up a slanting groove on the right.

First descent: Mr and Mrs G. Scott Johnston. 1948.

MEADOW FACE ROUTES

11. HANGING GULLY   250 feet   Very Difficult

A peripatetic route using the upper part of the gully
splitting the top left corner of the face. In its lower
reaches the gully becomes an exiguous crack guarded by
slimy slabs. Enter gully from the left by a disagreeable
downward traverse. Dispose of the remains of the gully
by a through route and gain grassy platform on right
wall. Take the left of two chimneys above and so emerge,

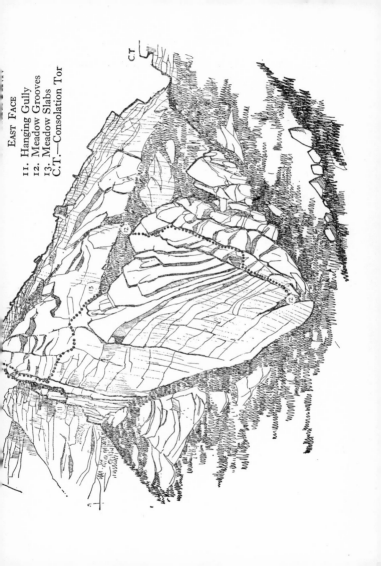

EAST FACE

11. Hanging Gully
12. Meadow Grooves
13. Meadow Slabs
C.T.—Consolation Tor

by a slabby shelf, on the arête forming the last section of
Route 13. *Not recommended.*

First ascent: G. C. Curtis, G. H. Townend, R. K. Fraser,
and H. K. Moneypenny. April 1944.

12. MEADOW GROOVES   400 feet   Very Difficult

This route follows grooves which run up the less steep
part of the face to the right of a remarkable series of
overlapping slabs. A heathery rake leads up to the point
where the rock begins to shake off its vegetatious blanket.
Start in groove farthest left.

(1) 80 feet. A big slab and a short groove lead up
towards two overlapping steps. Move to the right below
the latter to a belay underneath a 15 foot wall.

(2) 100 feet. Slant up wall from left to right (crux)
and step round into water-worn scoop which presents no
difficulties.

(3) 50 feet. Easy climbing to a tiny amphitheatre.

(4) 80 feet. Go up chimney on the right until forced
out to the right and continue upwards by twin narrow
chimneys.

(5) 90 feet. Follow through to a platform leading to
the Terrace (see Route 13). A further 150 feet of
climbing may be had by bearing left but this is rather
artificial.

First ascent: G. C. Curtis, H. K. Moneypenny and
E. J. W. Morrison. August 1944.

13. MEADOW SLABS   300 feet (approx.)   Difficult

A sloping grass shelf, called the Terrace, extends
leftwards from the upper slopes at the head of Ealta
Coire separating the precipitous lower face from a band
of high-angle slabs set below the main ridge. It peters
out some distance short of the blunt edge or ridge

capping the vertical section of the face. The route
follows the line of the blunt ridge. Walk up the grass of
the Terrace to a shallow crack with chock stones formed
by a slab leaning against the wall above. Climb crack
and then descend obliquely by turf ledges towards the
overhanging termination of the blunt ridge. Cross a
long slab and beyond will be seen a 10 foot chimney
with a chock stone.

(1) 30 feet. The little chimney soon narrows to a
crack and gives access to the crest.

(2) 30 feet. Climb interesting undercut chimney on
left.

(3) 30 feet. Continue in same line over easier rock.

(4) 60 feet. Move right and ascend grassy crack
leading to a branching chimney.

(5) 50 feet. Use left branch of chimney and climb
wall above by a slanting crack. Finish by a pull up on
the left and a short arête. Route 11 comes in on the left
at this point beyond which only scrambling remains.

First ascent: G. C. Curtis, H. K. Moneypenny and E. J.W.
Morrison. August 1944.

CONSOLATION TOR

Near the junction of the ridge running SE to Beinn a'
Chliabhain and the main Tarsuinn—A' Chir ridge there
is a small flat-topped mass of rock which provides a
number of climbing problems of surprising variety. The
quality of the rock is excellent.

14. TARSUINN No. 1 CHIMNEY   120 feet   Hard Severe

Below Consolation Tor there is a cyclopean buttress on
the slopes falling steeply into Coire Daingean. It contains two very deeply cut vertical chimneys numbered 1
and 2 from the left. A convenient path, connecting the

cols on either side, passes below the chimneys. Start
near the back of the chimney which penetrates 40 ft.
into the mountain. The first pitch is the crux.

First ascent: S.M.C. party in 1901.

15. TARSUINN No. 2 CHIMNEY 120 feet Severe

The first 15 feet consists of a thin crack. The difficulties
_re concentrated in this section, for above the chimney
widens and gives climbing of moderate standard.

In 1901 this chimney was explored from above and the
initial 15 feet declared to be "impossible".

First ascent: H. Grant, G. McKinley, C. McPherson,
        W. Russell, A. Slack and Mrs F. Grant. July 1941.

16. WOOLPACK ROUTE   120 feet   Difficult

This route goes up the cyclopean wall to the right of
No. 2 Chimney. Much variation is possible and the
finish can be made either by No. 2 or by an unnamed
chimney further right.

First ascent: unknown.

17. LOWER LEFT-HAND CHIMNEY   100 feet
                                      Difficult

This route lies in the area of slabs below the Tarsuinn
Chimneys. The start is marked by a patch of gravel
100 feet left of the foot of Boundary Gully. A 10 foot
crack is climbed to reach the foot of the chimney which
is formed by overlapping slabs.

First ascent: unknown.

BEINN A' CHLIABHAIN, 2217 feet

The only climb on this mountain so far recorded lies
on the most defined of several small buttresses outcrop-
ping high up on the Coire Daingean side. It is usually

approached by an oblique *descent* from the col between
Ealta Coire and Coire Daingean.

18. HAAKON'S HIGHWAY 260 feet Very Difficult

Begin a little to the right of the lowest point of the
central buttress and climb up to a large ledge (55 feet).
The route then keeps on the right-hand side in a series of
grooves and cracks to the final chimney which is strenuous and which contains some seemingly ill-jammed chock
stones. Although somewhat inconveniently situated this
is an entertaining little climb and well repays a visit.

First ascent: Mr and Mrs G. Scott Johnston. September
1945.

A' CHIR, 2335 feet

A' Chir (The Comb) is the culminating point of the
main ridge between Tarsuinn and Cir Mhor and is best
reached from Glen Rosa by (1) Coire Daingean, (2)
contouring the south-western slopes of Beinn a' Chliabhain and (3) the Cir Mhor—A' Chir col; and from
Glen Sannox by the Cir Mhor—Caisteal Abhail col.
The western face consists of an extensive area of slabs
(which may harbour some, as yet undiscovered, routes)
while on the east much steeper rock-faces plunge into
Coire Daingean and, further north, into the little Coire
Buidhe. The actual summit is a massive boulder which
can be scaled by at least three ways.

19. TRAVERSE OF A' CHIR RIDGE   Moderate

This interesting ridge scramble is justly celebrated as
one of the best in the British Isles. A good deal of
variation is possible but apart from one section immediately north of the famous gap or "mauvais pas" the
route is heavily scratched and unmistakable. Descending from the summit, heading north, the over-rated

mauvais pas occurs where the ridge levels out after a steep
step, turned on the western flank. A few yards beyond
on the right, descend a 15 foot wall leading to a grass
ledge which slants down out of sight. The sloping ledge
becomes a rock trench in its last few feet and brings one
out at a little col at the foot of an overhang which has
thus been turned. The succeeding ascent from the gap
is one of the best sections of the ridge. Just south of the
"mauvais pas" an exposed shelf leads down the face
into Coire Buidhe. The standard is moderate/difficult.

First traverse: Circa 1891.

COIRE DAINGEAN FACE

20. BOUNDARY RIDGE   380 feet   Difficult
                                    (Severe Variations)

This route follows the extreme left-hand edge of the
face and is not really a ridge in the usual sense of the
term. As the line of ascent is not always obvious a full
account is given.

Start at notch on crest reached by scrambling up 60
feet from bottom rocks.

(1) 70 feet. Climb slab to block on crest sporting a
bedstead knob. Mantleshelf up or swing round (left)
into grassy gully leading to a block belay.

(2) 70 feet. Follow 6 inch wide crack to large spike
set against wall on right.

(3) 70 feet. Climb wall above the spike and enter
another crack which conducts one to the foot of a steep
arête on the right.

(4) 60 feet. Move up arête to ledge, traverse a few
feet right and ascend steep slab and some broken ground
to a jumble of blocks on a platform overlooking Boundary
Gully. This platform may also be reached by a very

difficult chimney which is entered by traversing left towards Boundary Gully.

(5) 110 feet. Step up on to a long horizontal ledge running across the face and *follow it for 30 feet*. Surmount slab above and slant up left to wall with a little Y-shaped crack. Climb crack to broad rock shelf. A further 10 foot wall ends the climb.

Severe Variation A

Climb open corner behind the jumble of blocks at top of Pitch (4) and move with great difficulty on to shelf on the right. The Y-shaped crack lies a few feet above.

Severe Variation B

From platform below the open corner of Variation A a ledge runs across the vertical face above Boundary Gully. It quickly steepens and ends in a semi-detached flake noticeably overhanging. Follow ledge and surmount flake—a strenuous and exposed move. Move up right wall and mantleshelf on to terrace above to join original route.

First ascent of Original Route: G. C. Curtis and G. H. Townend (alternate leads); H. K. Moneypenny and H. J. Dunster (alternate leads). July 1943.

21. GULLY 3   300 feet   Difficult

This gully has the doubtful distinction of being the best in Arran. An enormous chock stone blocks the lower grassy section and entrance above this obstacle is gained by taking to a shattered basalt groove on the right wall from which a long stride leftwards round a bulge is made. The rest of the gully contains several short pitches.

First ascent: A. Arthur and H. MacRobert. July 1911.

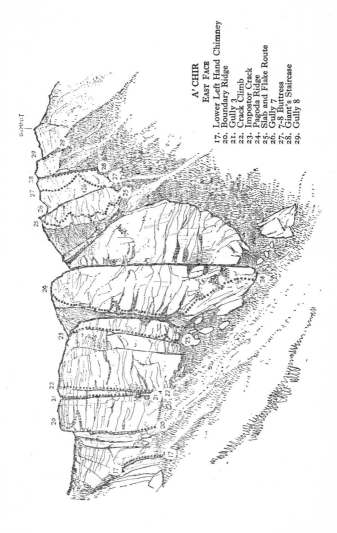

A' CHIR
EAST FACE

17. Lower Left Hand Chimney
20. Boundary Ridge
21. Gully 3
22. Crack Climb
23. Impostor Crack
24. Pagoda Ridge
25. Slab and Flake Route
26. Gully 7
27. 7-8 Buttress
28. Giant's Staircase
29. Gully 8

22. CRACK CLIMB   300 feet   Difficult

Begin as in Route 21, continuing up the collinear series of cracks which run up the face at a slightly divergent angle from the right-hand edge of Gully 3. A fair climb, lacking variety.

First ascent: H. MacRobert and W. A. Morrison. June 1908.

23. IMPOSTOR CRACK   300 feet   Very Difficult

As the name suggests this route is disappointing. It follows the prominent crack immediately left of Gully 4. At the overhang, traverse right to short chimney which leads back to the main crack. Above the chock stones, encountered well up the climb, take to the crack on the left wall and finish by an easy chimney further left.

First ascent: G. C. Curtis, G. H. Townend, H. K. Moneypenny and H. J. Dunster. July 1943.

Gully 4 contains only shattered basalt and grass.

24. PAGODA RIDGE   700 feet   Severe

This is the longest and best climb on the face. It does not by any means maintain its standard throughout but the "longueurs" which so often spoil Arran climbs are negligible. In the main, the route lies up the right-hand edge of Gully 4 and Pitches (1) and (2) may be omitted by a direct ascent to the "side belay" from which Pitch (3) begins. This course is *not* recommended, for the first two pitches are technically interesting. Start at the bottom right-hand side of the buttress just to the left of the terminal slab. An arrow has been scratched on the rock at the spot (not by the editor).

(1) 90 feet. Climb grassy crack which terminates in a sharp flake. Make a rather delicate leftward traverse

up to a patch of heather and go left across a slab to a stance beneath a pronounced overhang.

(2) 90 feet. Move up delicately on to a sloping shelf and follow to edge. 30 feet above there is a side belay.

(3) 60 feet. Follow edge (with one "dog leg" to the right) to a pile of blocks on the fringe of a large patch of heather.

(4) 60 feet. Climb wall above heather patch using a short crack. A further few feet leads to a good stance behind a large block overhanging the Gully.

(5) 30 feet. Cross slab above to a tiny niche with rock spikes on the right.

(6) 80 feet. (Crux). Swing round corner on the right and make a delicate traverse across a concave slab until the short wall above can be climbed (left to right). Go left to edge where a jammed flake provides a good belay.

(7) 110 feet. Go up crack above belay and follow edge which becomes a vertical wall. Surmount wall by grooves and blocks to belay between two large boulders.

(8) 180 feet. Follow crest of ridge to top. This section is only Moderate to Difficult in standard but very pleasant climbing.

First ascent: G. H. Townend and G. C. Curtis. May 1943.

Gully 5 is a walk apart from a repulsive pitch at the bottom.

Gully 6 is wide and grassy. A convenient means of access to Routes 25-29 from the main ridge.

25. SLAB AND FLAKE ROUTE   360 feet   Severe

The lower half of the buttress between Gully 6 and Gully 7 has some fine steep rock. The upper part however is traversed by numerous grass ledges and accordingly the quality of the climbing deteriorates.

(1) 30 feet. Begin at the bottom left-hand corner of

the enormous slab forming the foot of the buttress and climb up near left edge to a stance.

(2) 55 feet. Press up on to protruding hold above (very hard for short climbers) and then tread rightwards up slab until it is possible to incline leftwards to the edge near a very large triangular flake (thread belay).

(3) 30 feet. Climb left edge of flake and cross heather terrace to block belay. Alternatively go up using right edge of the flake which is more strenuous.

(4) 20 feet. Ascend cleft slanting rightwards behind a large flake. It contains a chock stone.

(5) 35 feet. From the top left edge of the flake step across on to the steep wall opposite (crux) and so gain the heather ledge above. Alternatively attack the wall from the highest point of the flake using an undercut crack (layback move). Go right along heather ledge *past* a thin crack to the foot of a ladder of pocket holds which conducts one to a curious "eye-hole" belay on the ledge above.

(6) 90 feet. Go up rising grass rake on right to a rocky shelf leading leftwards to another shelf. Move rightwards up a slab to a flake belay.

(7) 25 feet. Climb corner above belay to a wide boulder-strewn terrace crossing the latter to a spike belay on the wall behind (beneath a broken spur of rock).

(8) 35 feet. Surmount broken spur and the slab above it. Then traverse right to a block belay.

(9) 40 feet. A wall and a wide crack give access to a grass terrace leading to the top of the buttress.

First ascent: G. H. Townend, G. C. Curtis and H. J. Dunster. September 1943.

26. GULLY 7   300 feet   Moderate

A typically unpleasant Arran gully. Not recommended.

27. 7-8 BUTTRESS　　　250 feet　　　Very Difficult

This buttress is the least attractive on the A' Chir face and gives a very scrappy route. There is much vegetation. Reach the left-hand edge of the buttress by a through route from the foot of Gully 7. In 200 feet or so upward progress is barred by a flawless wall and this is avoided by a long traverse right and then back left to the original line.

Not recommended.

First ascent: G. C. Curtis, G. H. Townend and H. J. Dunster. September 1943.

28. GIANT'S STAIRCASE　　　240 feet　　Very Difficult

A well defined open corner or step runs up the middle of 7-8 Buttress. The route follows a series of chimneys in this feature. A good strenuous climb.

(1) 50 feet. Ascend chimney to grass ledge.

(2) 100 feet. From top of grass ledge enter another chimney and climb it until, in approx. 60 feet a traverse out to the right can be made. Now follow broad heather ledge back left to the original line.

(3) 40 feet. A strenuous chimney with small but adequate holds at the top.

(4) 50 feet. Start in the chimney but soon traverse out right over a slab to a heather patch. Climb another slab (steep) to the top.

The original route is described above but it is possible to take all the chimneys direct.

First ascent: G. H. Townend and H. J. Dunster. September 1943.

29. GULLY 8　　　200 feet　　　Difficult

This short gully gives two good, if rather artificial, pitches. Best reached by a leftward descent from main ridge above Route 28.

30. BIRTHDAY CHIMNEY   100 feet   Severe

This chimney lies roughly in the middle of the west face of the little buttress immediately south of the A' Chir—Cir Mhor col and contains a projecting block about one third of the way up.

Use a crack to reach a ledge below the projection which is turned on the left. Then return to the chimney and climb to the top.

First ascent: unknown.

31. LEANING BLOCK CHIMNEY   100 feet
Very Difficult

Between Birthday Chimney and the left edge of the buttress there is a conspicuous leaning block near the foot of a chimney terminating in a decaying scoop. Pass behind the block and go straight up. In 40 ft. the chimney narrows and finally terminates against a short wall. At this point go right to a large platform from which 20 ft. of easy rock lead to the top.

First ascent: J. M. Johnstone, W. Wallace and Miss G. Hamilton. Easter 1958.

CIR MHOR, 2618 feet

To the ordinary tourist Goat Fell is the only peak of consequence in Arran because it is the highest. From a mountaineer's point of view the supremacy of Cir Mhor is absolute. This pre-eminence lies not only in the quality of the South Face routes but in the lovely lines of the mountain as a whole. Unlike the vast majority of Scottish peaks it is aesthetically satisfying from every point in the compass owing to its Matterhorn-like detachment from its neighbours.

SOUTH FACE

The topography of this face is best studied from a distance. The massive lines of the South Ridge buttressing the Rosa Pinnacle dominate the scene. East of the Pinnacle, beyond a wide gully called Sub Rosa, lies the much less well defined Prospero Buttress with its diagonal basalt dyke bisection and to the west the Caliban Buttress-ridge is only a stone's throw from the great south-western slabs. Much further west, flanking a well defined open gully, there is a cyclopean-block buttress known as Cubic Ridge. Areas of slab break through the surface in all directions tending to obscure the outlines of the principal features. A fairly well defined path leads up into Fionn Coire at the foot of the face from the main Glen Rosa track just before it begins the gradual ascent to the Saddle (the col between the Rosa and Sannox Glens).

From Glen Sannox, follow path to the Saddle and descend into Glen Rosa until a traverse across the south-eastern slopes of Cir Mhor to Fionn Coire can be made. It is necessary to keep fairly low to avoid several belts of slabs.

32. CUBIC RIDGE   300 feet   Very Difficult

A variable route. On the left side of the ridge the rocks merge into the hillside providing innumerable "walk offs". Start at the left-hand side and gain a broad ledge on the crest by slabs and a short steep crack. A 50 foot crack is then climbed. Traverse right to a short wall above which a crack leads to a horizontal section. There is a shallow gap between this and the upper ridge, which, when seen from below, gives the top of the lower part of the ridge a tower-like appearance. Beyond the gap the rocks are more broken and about 150 feet of

easy climbing leads to the final steep wall furnished with
excellent holds.

First ascent: G. H. Townend and F. Foxcroft. September
   1944.

33. CALIBAN'S CREEP   500 feet   Difficult

An amusing route with some delightful situations.

(1) 100 feet. Below the square cut vertical wall of the
buttress there are several overlapping slabs. Gain the
highest of these from the right and pass round below the
left corner of the vertical wall to a belay among a pile of
boulders on the west flank.

(2) 50 feet. Move out to the shattered vertical corner
and make an exposed upward traverse round to the foot
of a chimney on the vertical face. Belay on chock stone.

(3) 50 feet. Climb chimney to reach a bollard belay
on the broad, gently inclined roof.

(4) 70 feet. Walk over slabs to crest of horizontal
ridge which terminates against a vertical wall. Escape
through narrow rock tunnel on right to a block belay
(the Creep).

(5) 30 feet. Follow rock ledge round on to the
precipitous east face and thence into a deeply cut
chimney.

(6) 30 feet. Up chimney which develops into an
enormous slit trench, to a stance below the lip.

(7) 170 feet of delightful scrambling completes the
climb.

Keep as close to the right-hand edge as possible.

First ascent: G. C. Curtis and G. H. Townend. July 1943.

34. GREEN GULLY   300 feet   Very Difficult

This Gully divides the Caliban ridge from the South
Ridge of Rosa Pinnacle. A disgusting 100 ft. slimy scoop

gives access to a fan-shaped grass slope hemmed in by
steep walls. It is preferable to use the rocks on the right
until one can traverse horizontally into the amphitheatre. From the latter, two exits of moderate standard
can be made.

(1) Climb the left branch gully leading to the upper
scrambling of Caliban's Creep either by a series of
through routes, or keep outside.

(2) Climb out by the steep grass slope on the right
(just beyond, i.e. left, of Fourth Wall) and after a short
rock pitch reach the Terrace.

Avoidance of this gully is strongly recommended.

First ascent: unknown.

ROSA PINNACLE

35. FOURTH WALL   400 feet   Mild Severe
                                   (Very Severe Variation)

So named because it was the last face of the Pinnacle
to be climbed. A pleasant route with considerable ex-
posure on its upper section.

(1) 60 feet. Start at cairn level with the big vertical
step on Caliban's Ridge. Follow grassy groove to a turf
platform.

(2). 60 feet. Follow steeper continuation of the groove
(layback start).

(3) 40 feet. Take to rib on left and go straight up.
(S.W. Slabs route now goes off to the right.)

(4) 40 feet. The fault now becomes grassy so keep
left to reach a large platform.

(5), (6) and (7) 120 feet. Cracks and grooves lead
to the top of a large plinth leaning against the face.

(8) 60 feet. Climb up chimney above the plinth a few
feet and using a small ledge on the right leave the
chimney and take to the wall. Go up 6 ft. and then

follow a descending traverse until the slab above can be climbed. A rightward step leads into an easy groove.

(9) 20 feet. Reach Terrace by easy rocks.

Variation

A more direct finish can be made by following the chimney above the plinth to its termination. The chock stone at the narrow section however is loose, rendering the final move most hazardous—*not recommended*.

First ascent: G. H. Townend and H. K. Moneypenny. August 1945 (after protracted gardening earlier in that year).

36. SOU-WESTER SLABS   340 feet   Very Difficult

Perhaps the most pleasurable route in Arran. The rock and situations in the upper part are superb.

(1), (2) and (3) 160 feet. Same as Route 35.

(4) 50 feet. Make descending traverse rightwards to open chimney-crack and climb this to a bollard belay.

(5) 50 feet. Using twin flake cracks "walk" up to the square cut edge of the tremendous slab and drop down to sloping stance beyond (thread belay).

(6) 50 feet. Move rightwards up another slab beneath a vast overhang to a belay in a horizontal scoop.

(7) 30 feet. Traverse under overhang and step round corner to large platform on the South Ridge beneath the Three Tier Chimney of Route 37. The upper part of this route should then be followed (nowhere more than Very Difficult), but if time is short, traverse right from the platform to join Route 40 and thence descend to Sub Rosa Gully.

First ascent: G. H. Townend, G. C. Curtis, H. Hore and M. H. J. Hawkins. September 1944.

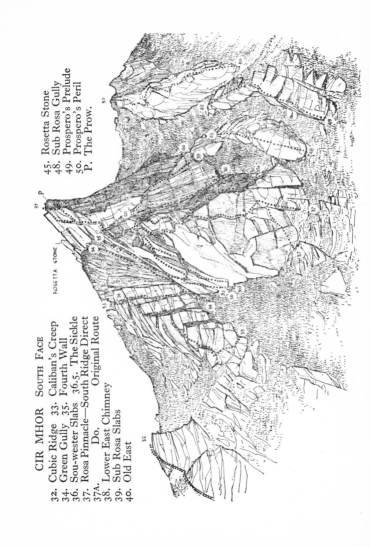

CIR MHOR   SOUTH FACE

32. Cubic Ridge 33. Caliban's Creep
34. Green Gully   35. Fourth Wall
36. Sou-wester Slabs 36.5. The Sickle
37. Rosa Pinnacle—South Ridge Direct
37A.   Do.   Original Route
38. Lower East Chimney
39. Sub Rosa Slabs
40. Old East

45. Rosetta Stone
48. Sub Rosa Gully
49. Prospero's Prelude
50. Prospero's Peril
P. The Prow.

36.5. THE SICKLE   250 feet   Hard Severe

This route follows a seemingly unpromising line up the great slabs to the right of route 36 and roughly parallel to it. It is deficient in sound belays and should only be attempted after a spell of dry weather. Rubbers recommended. It has a common start with Fourth Wall and Souwester Slabs. A little way up the initial groove of Routes 35 and 36 a broken ledge leads rightwards to a similar feature. Follow this to the foot of a short and rather slimy chimney. Block belay of sorts is available. Climb the chimney for 15 feet. One is then forced to take to the slab on the right. An upward traverse leads to a shallow scoop about 10 feet below two cracks which split the 3-foot thick bottom edge of the next higher slab. A piton should be used here for a running belay. Go straight up to a good stance in the cracks above the 3-foot wall. Follow the groove up the slab until, by using a series of micro-granite veins, a diagonal traverse rightwards can be made to the large platform immediately right of the huge overhang.

First ascent: J. H. Ashford and D. Burke. November 1957.

37. SOUTH RIDGE DIRECT 855 feet Very Severe

The finest route in Arran and considered among the best anywhere in the country. Choose a sunny day to savour its delights to the full.

From Coire Fionn one can pick out the elongated "S" crack running up the otherwise flawless vertical nose of the ridge which rises out of a jumble of slabs. The climbing really begins at a conspicuous rock crevasse 60 feet below and some way to the right of the "S" crack, level with the jammed blocks in Sub Rosa Gully. This point is best reached by an ascending traverse over slabs from the left (200 feet approx.) or more directly by a steep groove near Sub Rosa Gully.

(1) 60 feet. Climb up above the crevasse and follow a leftward trending groove to a horizontal ledge beneath the S crack (flake belay). (The left or west end of the ledge becomes a flake and by aiming at this point of arrival from the left a severe approach may be made (R. K. Fraser's variation).)

(2) 40 feet. Climb crack to a shelf with large triangular block belay.

(3) 25 feet. Surmount overhanging wall, using Y-shaped cracks. A hard move in a very airy situation.

(4) 20 feet. Continue up slabs to a block-strewn terrace.

(5) 100 feet. Traverse left across the top of a great slab to a side belay in the far corner.

(6) 60 feet. Layback up flake crack above and then make a delicate traverse rightwards across the foot of the upper slab until it is possible to move upwards to the wide platform above. Alternatively avoid the traverse by a layback all the way, using the undercut edge to the left of the upper slab (L. S. Lovat's extremely strenuous variation).

Pitches (5) and (6) can be avoided by a direct assault using the deeply cut chimney above the terrace (on right) or by traversing further round to the right and gaining the platform by an open scoop and wall on the east flank. Both variants are harder and much less interesting.

(7) 90 feet. Pull up into chimney above the platform. It is in three sections and leads to a belay on the crest of the ridge over two slabs separated by a short wall.

(8) 60 feet. Follow crest of well defined arête.

(9) 150 feet. Walk up to the sloping Terrace below the Upper Pinnacle which is seen to be a tilted stack of

vast granite sheets many feet thick. Adequate belays are sparse as the lengths of the following pitches indicate but stances may be taken at more frequent intervals as the leader may think fit.

(10) 90 feet. Gain the roof of the first slab by taking off from a conveniently placed flake a few yards left of the corner using excellent knob-like holds. Go straight up until a fault coming in on the left is reached. Follow this to its termination in a chimney (Spike belay).

(11) 40 feet. Climb chimney.

(12) 120 feet. The line of the chimney becomes a level grass ledge. Follow this until it is possible to climb on to the slab on the right. Go straight up to the crest. There is a stance of sorts at the corner of the next higher slab but no adequate belay. When the crest of the arête becomes holdless traverse on to the east face and reach the right-angled corner below the summit by treading an exposed outward sloping shelf. Climb crack in the corner, followed by a short slab to reach summit. Use horizontal crack below final slab for a belaying stance. (*Variation*: At the horizontal grass ledge continue up the fault to the foot of the next slab which leads straight up to the summit.)

First ascent: J. F. Hamilton and D. Paterson. 1941.

37a. SOUTH RIDGE ORIGINAL ROUTE 950 feet
Severe

(1) 60 feet. As in Route 37.

(2) 80 feet. Traverse right over easy ground until a recess on the right of the flawless wall containing the S crack can be entered. (This recess can also be reached more directly, if the right line is found, from Sub Rosa Gully.)

(3) 50 feet. Surmount the overhang and go up steep grass to a steep little wall. Climb this at the right or left

ROSA PINNACLE
East Face

sides to a ledge with a large triangular block belay. (This ledge leads round leftwards to the exit of the S crack.)

(4) 50 feet. Climb steep cracks above the ledge or traverse back into the corner and follow chimney to join Route 37 just short of the belay at the top of Pitch (4).

(5) to (12) as in Route 37, Pitch (6) being the crux.

First ascent: J. A. Ramsay and party. 1935.

38. LOWER EAST CHIMNEY 150 feet Very Difficult (Severe)

This indifferent route lies up an ill defined grassy chimney on the east flank of the South Ridge lower section. It has a large jammed block which one goes behind. Keep in the chimney until a left traverse can be made to the block-strewn terrace at the top of Pitch (4) of Route 37 (Severe) which has then to be followed. The route is therefore a disagreeable variation and is not recommended.

First ascent: unknown.

39. SUB ROSA SLABS   100 feet   Difficult

Start at grassy neck projecting into Sub Rosa Gully near the bottom right hand corner of the slabby *lower* east face and climb a succession of slabs divided by two grassy bands to join Route 40 below the wall of the Upper Pinnacle.

First ascent: unknown.

40. OLD EAST   200 feet   Moderate

A convenient means of passage from Sub Rosa Gully to the Terrace and vice versa. From the Gully start as close to the precipitous wall of the Upper Pinnacle as possible. Go straight up for 15 feet and incline leftwards passing beneath an overhang (this section can be slimy in damp conditions). Hug the base of the cliff until a little chimney is seen ahead. Ascend the steep slab to its left on magnificent holds and scramble over and round some large boulders to the Terrace. Anyone wishing to ascend the Rosa Pinnacle from Fionn Coire on rock nowhere more than difficult in standard should link Prospero's Prelude, Old East and the Upper South Ridge (Pitches (10) to (12) of Route 37).

First ascent: unknown.

ROSA PINNACLE EAST FACE

The key feature of this splendidly steep face is the slightly overhanging edge which sweeps down from the summit like a ship's prow. A collinear series of vertical fissures goes down the face to the bottom from the Prow and marks the general line of Labyrinth. A similar but less well defined line of cracks and chimneys runs parallel some 30 feet to the right and is used by Easter Route. Yet another system of fissures in a plane at right angles to those mentioned above begins as a prominent chimney-crack near the SE corner and continues across the face to intersect Labyrinth beneath the Prow.

41. MINOTAUR   175 feet   Very Severe

At the SE corner of the Upper Pinnacle a prominent crack runs vertically upwards to terminate near the Eyrie. Its plane is parallel to the upper edge of South Ridge. From Sub Rosa Gully scramble up to a little grass platform below the right-angled corner where the crack makes an exiguous beginning.

(1) 30 feet. Climb the crack, the first few feet are

very strenuous, to a cushion of heather below the point where an overhang develops. There is a piton in the left wall.

(2) 35 feet. The next overhanging section is exceedingly strenuous until about 10 feet up it is possible to get the body into the crack (slim bodies only). A runner may be fixed round a chock-stone at this point. By jamming (face left) continue up the chimney until it is possible to move out on to the rib on the left. This leads to the wider upper chimney where there is an excellent belay.

(3) 110 feet. Straight up chimney which gradually widens to the proportions of a gully and exit on right of large boulder.

The grass patch above Pitch 4 of Labyrinth is reached by a short scramble over the rock-rib on the right.

First ascent: D. McKelvie and D. Sim. August 1958.

42. LABYRINTH   400 feet   Very Difficult

A varied, interesting route, strongly recommended. Entrance to the Labyrinth is by a "close" below the right-hand termination of the monolithic wall above Sub Rosa Gully.

(1) 70 feet. Scramble up sloping bed of the "close" or chimney and climb out through vent on the left (or right). Continue up to a grassy platform against the monolithic wall.

(2) 30 feet. Climb corner and succeeding chimney to a cockpit with large block belay.

(3) 50 feet. Continue up chimney to a sloping patch of grass. A horizontal ledge runs across the wall on the left. Using the ledge for the hands, make a delightful traverse left into a little corner under an overhang. *Piton* belay only.

(4) 40 feet. (crux). Climb straight up (wide straddle for short limbed climbers) to sloping grass terrace. Skirt wall on right and enter deep chimney where a block belay will be found.

(5) 30 feet. Go vertically upwards and emerge on grass platform.

(6) 30 feet. The route goes *behind* the chock stones seen above and leads to a little rock balcony, the Eyrie, delightfully situated under the Prow.

(7) 40 feet. From the Eyrie step rightwards beneath the Prow into the bottom of a long crack. Keep traversing right by means of a narrow ledge until easier ground gives access to a broad grassy rake.

(8) 80 feet. Follow rake via a tiny chimney to a cluster of enormous blocks.

(9) 30 feet. Drop down beyond blocks and enter steep chimney overlooking Pinnacle Gully. A slab above the chimney leads to the top.

First ascent: G. C. Curtis and H. K. Moneypenny. September 1943.

42a. STEWART ORR'S VARIATION   135 feet
Hard Severe

(7a) 35 feet. From the Eyrie continue straight up over easy rock to a spacious corner.

(8a) 100 feet. On the east wall there is a curious flange. Layback on this until the right foot can be jammed in the corner crack and thence make a landing on the ledge above. Traverse left along the ledge and swing round a bulge. A 10 ft. slab leads to the South Ridge at a point a few yards before the delicate traverse of Pitch (12).

First ascent: J. Stewart Orr and J. C. MacLaurin. May 1951.

43. EASTER ROUTE   335 feet   Hard Severe

A good direct route with a fine finish. Begin approximately 30 feet. from the right-hand corner of the wall and about the same distance to the right of Route 42.

(1) 60 feet. Easy climbing to large leaning block at the bottom of a chimney-crack.

(2) 70 feet. Follow crack to grass ledge with blocks.

(3) 30 feet. Continue up chimney to another patch of grass (from this point Route 42 may be joined on the left at Pitch (3) and on the right a ledge with a large block leads into Pinnacle Gully).

(4) 40 feet. Climb vertical chimney above until a move out rightwards to a stepped ledge can be made. The ledge bears a large sloping cap of turf.

(5) 40 feet. From the ledge move up wall to reach horizontal cracks which are followed leftwards to the edge. Then go straight up to a grass ledge.

(6) 25 feet. Traverse left to a belay at the bottom of a well defined crack which curves upwards to the right of the Prow (the "Eyrie" of Route 42 lies a few feet to the left).

(7) 40 feet. Go up curving crack (face right).

(8) 30 feet. Continue up chimney-crack to exit on summit ledge.

First ascent: K. Barber and S. Pigott. Easter 1938.

43a. DOUBLE CRACK VARIATION   Severe

On the Pinnacle Gully face of Rosa Pinnacle there is a prominent right angled corner some 30 feet high. Both walls are split by vertical cracks of convenient width for jambing feet and arms. By this means one gains the "cap of turf" at the top of Pitch 4 on Easter Route which is then followed. Although this variant shortens the climb by 150 feet it gives an entertaining route of sus-

RCIA D

tained difficulty apart from the easy traverse called
Pitch 6.

First ascent: W. Wallace and J. M. Johnstone. June 1958.

44. KEYHOLE CRACK (NORTH FACE)   100 feet
Very Difficult

Between Rosa Pinnacle and the summit rocks of Cir
Mhor there is a little buttress falling into the upper bay of
Sub Rosa Gully. Pinnacle Gully is the grassy boulder-
strewn slope between this mass of rock and the north
face of the Pinnacle. Halfway up the Gully a vertical
chimney-crack will be seen on the left. The first few feet
are awkward as the rock is somewhat decayed. Finish
by tunnelling under the large boulders near the top.

First ascent: E. Banner-Mendus and G. P. Pinder. May
     1946.

45. ROSETTA STONE   Very Severe

This vast block lies on the west side of the Pinnacle
beyond the top of Pinnacle Gully. It is only amenable to
attack on one side and this requires considerable deter-
mination and powers of adhesion. A rope can be thrown
over the top for protection.

First ascent (free): R. Smith. May 1957.
First ascent (aided): J. Maclay and W. W. Naismith 1894.

Easy Route to top of Rosa Pinnacle

From the south side of the Rosetta Stone two large
slabs lead to the summit. Climb the first by a diagonal
crack on the left and use the trench-like chimney
splitting the second to reach the top. Numerous opportunities for short climbs on fine rough slabs exist in this
area. The 60 foot slab left of the easy route to the summit was climbed by E. Banner-Mendus and Miss M.
Hargreaves in May 1946. Standard Very Severe.

46. RUDDY KNUCKLES 150 feet Severe

This direct and strenuous route uses a crack running up a well defined corner on the south wall of Pinnacle Gully Buttress. The start is almost level with the escape traverse at the top of Pitch (3) of Easter Route. A large square block forms a platform beneath the corner. Gain this either by its left or right side. Thereafter keep in the corner crack until near the top when one may finish either by a pull up on the left wall or by a through route.

First ascent: unknown.

46.5. PINNACLE GULLY BUTTRESS 170 feet
Very Difficult

The east face of this little buttress consists of a series of walls and ledges. Start at the first wall where a detached slab projects above it. Thereafter keep as close to the centre as possible. The final wall should be taken direct but an easier way will be found up its right hand edge. The climb is artificial in so far as escape is possible to the right at one or two points.

First ascent: W. Wallace and J. M. Johnstone. June 1958.

47. BRODICK CHIMNEY 150 feet Difficult

This indifferent climb is to be found on the gable wall at the foot of the Cir Mhor summit rocks (south side) a few yards right of the tourist path. It is much the most prominent fissure of several seaming the wall.

First ascent: unknown.

48. SUB ROSA GULLY Easy/Moderate

This broad depression between the eastern flank of Rosa Pinnacle and the low buttress-ridge of Prospero is split into two branches in its lower section by a broad ramp of slabs. The true right branch has a little pitch formed by jammed boulders at its foot but otherwise is mainly of grass and gravel. The true left branch is an unpleasant compost of loose boulders, scree, slime and heather. The slabs between them give 200 feet or so of moderate to difficult climbing according to the line taken and are to be preferred when ascending from Fionn Coire. The upper half of the Gully consists of boulder-strewn grass.

First ascent: unknown.

49. PROSPERO'S PRELUDE   400 feet (approx.)
Moderate/Difficult

The low ridge of rocks forming the eastern boundary of Sub Rosa Gully is roughly halved by a short diagonal basalt gully not visible from below. The lower half is much broken and generally at an easy angle. The upper part rises precipitously above the diagonal gully and has steep walls on both flanks.

Begin near the water course draining the eastern branch of Sub Rosa Gully and keep to the crest as much as possible. There are one or two amusing little pitches but the rest is scrambling. Traverses into Sub Rosa Gully can be made at several points and the route is recommended as an approach to the climbs on the east face of Rosa Pinnacle. (See also Route 40.)

First ascent: H. K. Moneypenny and G. C. Curtis. September 1943.

50. PROSPERO'S PERIL   440 feet   Hard Severe

A fine route giving varied climbing. The extreme toe of the buttress is in an advanced state of decay, otherwise the rock is excellent.

(1) 60 feet. The first objective is a horizontal ledge on the crest above a little vertical wall (undercut). *Either* start below wall and traverse obliquely rightwards to a scoop *or* climb the latter from the bottom. The scoop leads to the little ledge on the crest. A short groove then goes up to a concave slab. Traverse upwards to the left edge of the slab and go straight up to a commodious grass ledge by an open corner (Crux). Alternatively traverse right from the concave slab into the upper part of a chimney-crack which leads to the grass ledge. (*Note:* The foot of this chimney lies a few feet to the right of the initial scoop and can be used as an alternative, more strenuous start. A rock spike near the chimney can be lassoed to give the leader some protection.)

(2) 40 feet. Walk round corner on right and climb undercut chimney.

(3) 80 feet. Easy climbing to large boulder-strewn ledge.

(4) 70 feet. Climb scoop on the left until a short traverse right to the foot of a curving flake crack can be made. Layback to crest of the arête. Take to the right wall for a few feet and then go up to a tiny niche. Follow inclined ledge to a spike belay under an overhanging block.

(5) 40 feet. Surmount slab-wall on left by 6 inch crack (awkward exit from overhang) and climb slab to large knob belay below a right-angled corner.

(6) 100 feet. Gain large slab by right-angled corner (10 feet) and follow grassy groove. A patch of grass then leads to the wall-edge of the final slab which is split by a little chimney (belay).

(7) 50 feet. Surmount overhanging chock stone and step up into cleft above. 20 feet of easy climbing brings one to the top of the buttress.

First ascent: G. H. Townend and G. C. Curtis. July 1943.

NORTH GOAT FELL, 2684 feet

On the SW slope below the summit there is a considerable area of slabs but as yet no continuous route over them has been found. Near the right-hand edge a moderate route can be had. There are also some short scrambles up the little buttresses falling in the direction of Glen Rosa from the tors between North Goat Fell and Goat Fell itself. There is nothing to justify a specific visit and mention is made of this area for those who wish to enliven their ridge walk.

GOAT FELL, 2866 feet

ROSA SLABS

51. EVENING TRAVERSE   800 feet   Mild Severe

From the Glen Rosa track one gets a fore-shortened view of the vast area of slabs plating the western slope of Goat Fell. A small hanging corrie lies beyond the right-hand edge of the slabs. Aim for the water course draining this depression. Unmistakable landmarks on the face are so few that it was felt desirable to give a detailed account of this climb. Previous routes were made up the Slabs in 1945 and 1946 by parties led by Dr J. H. B. Bell and Mr J. Jenkins but their precise line has not been recorded in sufficient detail to establish with any certainty which sections are common to all. The wide expanse of rock below the main grass terrace is open to much variation, whereas the upper section is not.

The climb begins at the lowest slab, a huge undercut specimen lying to the left of the water course.

(1) 100 feet. Go round top of undercut slab and head for a crescent-shaped eave (formed by the overlap of one slab on another) which will be seen on the "port bow".

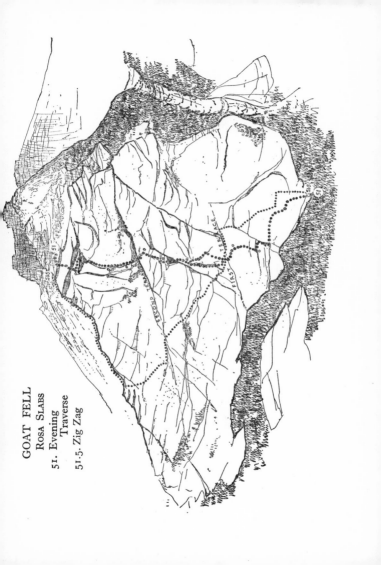

GOAT FELL
ROSA SLABS

51. Evening
    Traverse

51.5. Zig Zag

(2) 80 feet. Climb up to the right of the "crescent" and traverse left above it into a shallow scoop bounded on the left by the edge of a steep slab.

(3) 60 feet. From a horizontal shelf below the steep slab, climb up an incipient groove a few feet from its right edge. Move right when groove finishes and reach top on small holds. Then traverse left a few feet to a rounded spur of rock. Beyond the spur there is a stance in a little niche.

(4) 70 feet. Follow the shallow scoop above the niche to more broken ground on the left and so reach the First Terrace—an ill defined rake running diagonally across the face from left to right.

(5) 80 feet. 60 feet above the First Terrace, a projecting boss of rock shaped like a pillbox will be noticed. Take to the slabs coming down to the right of the pillbox and aim for a grass ledge aligned towards the latter. Traverse left (from the grass ledge) across intervening slab on tiny holds and skirt the right-hand side of the pillbox to reach a large block belay above it.

(6) 70 feet. Scramble up easy ground to an overhanging edge which slants up rightwards.

(7) 50 feet. Surmount overhang by a convenient crack and move up slab to a small spike belay.

(8) 100 feet. Trend leftwards over easy ground to reach the well defined Second Terrace in 30 feet. A series of cracks and grooves rises above the Second Terrace to a small platform bearing a large flake, shaped like a grave stone, which makes a good thread belay.

(9) 60 feet. Enter groove above the "grave stone" and go straight up to a pile of blocks lying below the wall-like edge of the enormous slab on the left.

(10) 70 feet. Twin "dièdres" one set below the other lead upwards. Traverse into the lower and layback up it. When the corner crack gives out an excellent hold

for the left hand turns up. Adequate holds lead to a little wall. Move up wall and cross slab above to a spike belay.

(11) 60 feet. The overlapping edges of the huge slabs above form two overhanging walls. The first is easy and the second is tackled by using a flake to the right of a sharp projection. This move finishes the climb.

From the top of the slabs a broken ridge of large blocks leads up in the direction of the summit.

First ascent of Rosa Slabs: J. H. B. Bell, G. A. Collie and
  C. C. Gorrie. May 1945
First ascent of Evening Traverse: J. M. Johnstone and W. C.
  Harrison (alternate leads). August 1955.

51.5. ZIG ZAG   935 feet   Severe

This interesting route is divided into two parts by a very long traverse and a walk *down* the grassy Second Terrace. The first section, though having a common start with Evening Traverse, pursues a line more to the right while the second for the most part is located on or near the left-hand edge of the slab area.

(1) 60 feet. Start as for route 51. Go straight up steep slab to more broken ground.

(2) 70 feet. Climb broken slab to a 3 feet wall with an undercut crack running out to the left. Using crack (lay-back) traverse left for 30 feet then up over shelf to a small terrace.

(3) 40 feet. Move up slab towards a small grass gully on the left. Standing belay only.

(4) 40 feet. Using the right-hand wall of the gully go straight up to a belay on the First Terrace.

(5) 350 feet approx. By the line of least resistance, traverse leftwards to reach the Second Terrace, which is *descended* to the point where a small crack gives access to the slabs above.

(6) 50 feet. Gain the face of the slab by the small crack and follow a line of good holds to a ledge with a waterslide on the left and a large flake above.

(7) 30 feet. Traverse rightwards below flake to a block belay.

(8) 15 feet. Reach top of the flake by a delicate traverse leftwards.

(9) 30 feet. Follow crack above the flake to edge overlooking grassy gully.

(10), (11) and (12) 240 feet. Keep on edge of slabs all the way to a grass terrace marking the upper limit of the whole slab-face. A further 100 feet or so of climbing may be had on the broken buttress-ridge above this point.

First ascent: D. McKelvie and D. Sim. June 1958.

PART II

GLEN SANNOX BASIN

CIOCH NA H-OIGHE, 2168 feet

This shapely mountain is the northern termination of the main ridge connecting the eastern peaks. A deeply carved corrie, commonly called the Devil's Punch Bowl, gives access to the precipitous eastern face, which despite its high angle is festooned with vegetation. Much of the rock is unsound, and where it is good, as in the great bastion in the middle of the face, too steep and unflawed to be climbable. Five ledges roughly parallel to one another run diagonally across the face from left to right. They are composed of grass, heather and mainly rotten rock and despite the fine airy situations of their upper reaches they are best avoided. The proximity of the mountain to Sannox makes a summer evening visit quite feasible, hence the names given to the two routes on the NE face.

LEDGES 1-5

Attempts have been made to grade the notorious Cioch na h-Oighe ledges in order of difficulty. In view of the objective dangers inherent in a traverse of any one of them, this seems an insoluble problem. Who can know when a heather hold will give way or a handhold crumble? They contain so little rock, bad or otherwise, that they can hardly be considered as rock climbing routes. This reference to them is therefore intended as a *warning* to the unwary.

52. 1896 ROUTE   500 feet (approx.)   **Difficult**

Start near foot of No. 3 Ledge and climb slabby rocks
and grass to No. 4 Ledge. Follow No. 4 Ledge until
under the summit of the mountain. Strike up cleaner
rocks above the ledge to emerge a short distance from
the cairn. There is too much grass and heather climbing
to make this route satisfactory.

First ascent: W. P. Haskett-Smith and W. W. Naismith.
     1896.

53. COXON'S ROUTE   300 feet   Very Difficult

Near the start of No. 2 Ledge the rocks above it overhang. Get above and a little right of this overhanging
section by ascending easy rocks and heather on its left.
Go straight up 60 feet to a belay at the right-hand end of
a heathery ledge. Now follow the narrow ledge leftwards
and then go up to a corner with a jammed flake on the
wall right of it. Climb the wall via the flake and reach a
good block belay by a short traverse leftwards. Continue
to traverse left for a few feet and move up a steep slab
to gain an easy groove which gives access to No. 3
Ledge below the great vertical bastion (unclimbable)
between Nos. 3 and 4 Ledges. Further progress involves
following No. 3 Ledge either up or down.

First ascent: L. S. Coxon, G. S. Bower and A. S. Pigott.
     April 1938.

54. MIDNIGHT RIDGE DIRECT   270 feet
                                   Very Severe

Where the slabby northern slope of the mountain
meets the east face a well defined edge or ridge is formed.
The bottom section is vertical and thereafter the angle
lessens steadily to become moderate at the exit from
No. 1 Ledge. From the lip of Coire na Ciche go straight

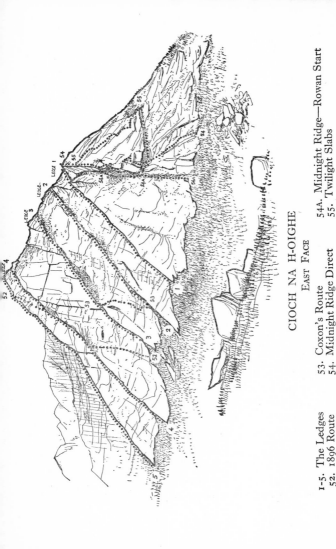

CIOCH NA H-OIGHE
EAST FACE

1-5. The Ledges	54A. Midnight Ridge—Rowan Start
52. 1896 Route	55. Twilight Slabs
53. Coxon's Route	
54. Midnight Ridge Direct	

up to the "nose" of the ridge by 150 feet of difficult vegetatious slabs and grooves. Just right of the corner there is a little recess with a thread belay.

(1) 30 feet. Climb overhanging crack to a broad sloping ledge. Move up 7-foot wall on small holds to a grass platform. Thread belay on wall behind or use a piton.

(2) 15 feet. (crux). From the left edge of the grass platform go round the corner by mantleshelving on to the undercut sloping slab (most awkward) which leads to a commodious ledge. A running belay (line) can be threaded at the corner. There is a spike belay 8 ft. above the ledge.

(3) 30 feet. Swing round vertical rib on the left, climb crack above for 15 feet and then scale right wall to a small ledge with a floor belay.

(4) 30 feet. Climb crack on the right and then bear left over broken blocks to a large platform.

(5) 15 feet. Go up a scoop to reach the crest of the arête.

(6) and (7) 150 feet. Follow the arête to open ground.

First ascent: G. H. Townend and G. C. Curtis. May 1944.

54*a*. MIDNIGHT RIDGE (ROWAN TREE START)
200 feet   Difficult

This route joins the Direct one above its severe sections and presumably the first ascent was made as a reconnaissance for the integral route achieved a week later.

From the start of the Direct Route enter the shallow gully on the left of the ridge and go up to a rowan tree. From the latter go right and descend slightly on a rock ledge until one can climb up to a large platform—the top of Pitch (4) on the Direct Route which is then followed.

First ascent: G. H. Townend, G. C. Curtis, H. K. Moneypenny and R. K. Fraser. April 1944.

55. TWILIGHT SLABS   300 feet   Severe

To reach the start follow the sloping mossy ledge below Midnight Ridge to the right until an incipient gravelly gully is reached. There is a triangular overhang at the head of the gully which is descended a few feet to begin the climb by the slabs on its right.

(1) 60 feet. Go up slabs and then traverse left (above triangular overhang) to a patch of heather (piton belay necessary).

(2) 70 feet. Climb slab on left by a flanking move and at its apex go straight up a wall to the foot of a little rock arête. There is an insecurely jammed block at the base of the arête. Follow scoop running up to the right of the arête to a heathery terrace.

(3) 60 feet. Gain the large slab above by the split block under it and traverse holdless rock to an incipient groove which leads to a large projecting boulder. (Thread belay behind boulder.)

(4) 110 feet. Traverse left 20 feet and climb up left edge of slabs to reach Midnight Ridge (about 50 feet from the top).

Note: From the finish of Midnight Ridge the best route of descent is by the slabby face further north of Twilight Slabs. With a little care a straightforward line can be found. If it is too dark to see any distance ahead, traverse round towards Glen Sannox until contact with the tourist path is made.

First ascent: G. C. Curtis and Miss F. M. King. July 1944.

56. TRAVERSE OF SUMMIT RIDGE   Easy

The scramble along the well defined ridge connecting Cioch na h-Oighe to the broad mass of Mullach Buidhe is quite pleasant especially if one keeps on the crest all the way.

MULLACH BUIDHE—NORTH GOAT FELL,
2688 feet

On the Sannox face of Mullach Buidhe extensive sheets of slab break through the heather. They are usually wet and, being roughly in the middle of the slopes, hardly justify a special visit. Neither do the numerous outcrops round the rim of Coire nam Fuaran. They provide short climbs most conveniently reached from the summit ridges.

CIR MHOR

As one walks up Glen Sannox the North-East Face looks magnificient and seems to promise many fine long rock climbs. A wedge of grass tapers diagonally across the face from the broad shoulder east of the summit pyramid to the high Coire na h-Uaimh. The LOWER FACE is built of high-angle overlapping slabs and except for the section directly beneath the grass wedge has so far proved impregnable to attack. The UPPER FACE is steep but much more broken, being intersected by innumerable grass ledges. It may be said at once that not one first-class route has yet been discovered on the entire face. The best combination is probably B2-C Rib—Bow Window Cave—Bell's Groove.

Coire na h-Uaimh, at the foot of the face, is most easily reached from Glen Sannox by branching right from the main path, before it begins the ascent to the Saddle, and following an ill defined track on the true left bank of the burn. At the water slide below the lip of the corrie keep well left. From the Saddle, climb up to the rocks of the LOWER NE FACE and descend the slope beside them until it is possible to skirt the slabs on the left. *Avoid the grassy ledge leading into the middle of the face.* Keep contouring leftwards and so join the Glen Sannox route below the rim of the corrie.

LOWER N.E. FACE

Gully A. Unclimbed.

57. GULLY B1   400 feet   Difficult

Apart from two pitches in the lower section, the bed of the gully is mainly of grass. In 1903, F. S. G. Goggs and Bennett Gibbs, who apparently didn't like the look of the second pitch, took to the rocks above the left wall and reached the top by a devious route.

First ascent (integral): G. C. Curtis and H. K. Moneypenny. June 1942.

58. GULLY B2   450 feet   Very Difficult

Start in B1 Gully and above the first pitch, follow the branching gully to the right which finishes in a large cave. Turn the cave on the right wall. Above, the gully is mainly steep grass with a blocked up exit. The latter is known as BOTTLE DUNGEON CAVE. It is customary to make one's escape by combined tactics. The Cave may be avoided by climbing on to the rib between B2 and B1 Gullies some distance below the exit as was done in 1912 by Messrs MacRobert, Raeburn, Young and Miss Raeburn.

First ascent: Messrs W. Wickham King, Evers and Bristow. 1892.

59. B2-C RIB   240 feet   Very Difficult

This is probably the best climb on the NE Face. The rib consists of a series of slabs and ledges. Belays are scarce but stances are adequate. The route follows the line of least resistance. There is a good belay in the niche to the left of the final overhang. Move out a few feet from the niche and then go straight up using an undercut hold to support the body while locating the excellent

RCIA E

hold over the top. In 1952 (Easter) T. Wallace and D.
Gilchrist made the following variation. About 100 ft.
from the start they traversed left to the edge of the rib
where good holds led up to an excellent belay on a
heather ledge. They then found themselves at the pitch
below the overhang.

The usual finish is by B2 Gully and Bottle Dungeon
Cave. Alternatively trend rightwards and use the final
section of Gully C to reach open ground.

First ascent: Messrs J. H. Bell, Boyd, Green and Napier.
July 1895.

Gully C. Unclimbed. (In 1904 W. A. Morrison and
party ascended the topmost section of the Gully after
climbing B2-C Rib.)

60. GULLY D (Trap Dyke Climb) 300 feet Moderate

This obvious line of weakness should be avoided—a
most unpleasant route.

First ascent: W. W. Naismith and W. Douglas. 1894.

UPPER N.E. FACE

This includes everything above and to the right of the
grass wedge beginning beyond the slabs right of Gully D
and slanting up leftwards. The Wedge provides an easy
route from Coire na h-Uaimh to the east ridge of the
mountain.

61. STONESHOOT RIDGE   400 feet   Moderate

This is the grassy ridge between the Wedge and the
Eastern Stoneshoot. Start at the bottom of the latter and
gain the ridge by decaying rocks. There is no difficulty
in following its crest all the way—a dreary route.

First ascent: Messrs J. H. Bell and Green. 1894.

62. BOW WINDOW CAVE   Difficult

Above and to the left of the top of Stoneshoot Ridge a
gravelly defile leads up to a large cave formed by huge
jammed boulders. Access is equally easy from the Wedge.
Finding a way out through the roof provides some
amusement.

First ascent: W. W. Naismith and W. Douglas. 1894.

63. SUMMIT CHIMNEY   100 feet   Moderate

Just right of the grassy neck at the top of the Eastern
Stoneshoot a well cut chimney runs up the steep east face
of the summit rocks. Follow the line of least resistance.

First ascent: unknown.

64. BELL'S GROOVE   200 feet   Difficult

An interesting route, finishing almost on the summit.
Descend about 100 feet from the top of the Eastern
Stoneshoot and climb up into a grassy bay on the left.
Climb the short chimney at the back and go up behind
a huge block. Continue upwards to a level grass platform
behind which a chimney-crack slants up leftwards. This
is the famous Groove. Its ascent requires considerable
effort. The rest of the route is obvious.

First ascent: Messrs J. H. Bell and Green. 1894.

65. NAISMITH AND HASKETT-SMITH'S ROUTE
220 feet   Moderate

This upward traverse across the summit gable uses a
line of weakness running parallel to the approach to
Bell's Groove but some distance below it. It brings one
out west of the summit. Of little interest as a rock climb
but the situations are fine.

First ascent: W. W. Naismith and W. P. Haskett-Smith,
1896.

RCIA E*

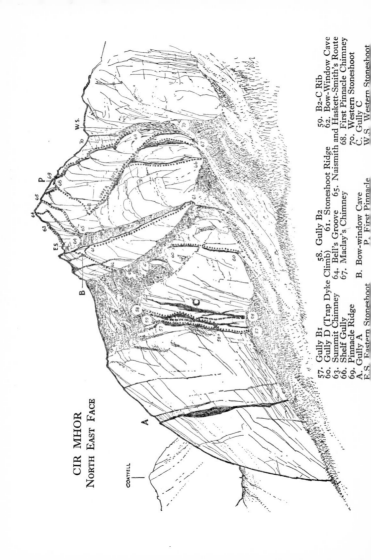

CIR MHOR
NORTH EAST FACE

57. Gully B1
60. Gully D (Trap Dyke Climb)
63. Summit Chimney
66. Shelf Gully
A. Gully A
E.S. Eastern Stoneshoot

58. Gully B2
61. Stoneshoot Ridge
64. Bell's Groove
67. Maclay's Chimney
B. Bow-window Cave
P. First Pinnacle

59. B2-C Rib
62. Bow-Window Cave
65. Naismith and Haskett-Smith's Route
68. First Pinnacle Chimney
70. Western Stoneshoot
C. Gully C
W.S. Western Stoneshoot

66. SHELF GULLY   300 feet   Difficult

This repulsive gully is the first break in the sweep of unclimbable rock to the right of the Eastern Stoneshoot. It leads to the prominent Upper Shelf which runs obliquely across the Upper Face from the foot of the Western Stoneshoot.

First ascent: unknown.

First descent: W. W. Naismith and W. P. Haskett-Smith, 1896.

67. MACLAY'S CHIMNEY   250 feet   Severe

One supposes that the vegetatious blanket covering this horrid scoop is now more formidable than it was in 1894 when the first ascent was made, for it was then described as a "difficult" route to the Upper Shelf.

First ascent: J. Maclay, W. Douglas and W. W. Naismith, 1894.

UPPER SHELF

This sloping terrace fades out at both ends and is well defined in its central section only. To reach it from the Western Stoneshoot involves a hazardous traverse at the top of Maclay's Chimney and possibly the least dangerous approach is by the rib between this Chimney and Shelf Gully; or, better still, by roping down on to it if a suitable hitch can be found on the western approach to Pinnacle Ridge. The upper extremity fades out into steep rocks in an advanced state of decay which precludes access from the Eastern Stoneshoot. The great plinth of rock about 100 feet high buttressing Pinnacle Ridge is the outstanding feature on the Upper Shelf. Further up (left of the plinth) a break in the steep rock wall behind the Shelf occurs and allows one to scramble up the face to the gap below the terminal tower of Pinnacle Ridge.

68. FIRST PINNACLE CHIMNEY   150 feet
Very Difficult

A series of chimneys seam the eastern flank of Pinnacle Ridge. This route follows the one finishing in the deep gap between the First and Second Pinnacles. From the grassy recess below the breach in the face above the Upper Shelf move up into the "blocked" foot of the chimney and go up to a jammed flake. Use the twin cracks above to reach the easy final section which leads to the narrow gap.

First ascent: J. M. Johnstone and Miss E. Wrench. May 1958.

69. PINNACLE RIDGE   450 feet   Difficult

Looking at the NE face from Coire na h-Uaimh one would not suspect that a ridge containing four pinnacles lay above the Upper Shelf. The great bastion of rock halfway along the Shelf marks the lower termination of the ridge for the first pinnacle caps it. Stepped ramps of rock and grass slope down to the Western Stoneshoot from the NW flank of the ridge and form the usual way of approach. The lowest ramp is probably the least unpleasant and by keeping as near to the drop on the left side as possible some excellent rock is found for the last 50 feet or so to the first pinnacle. The bold can leap from the topmost block across the narrow gap between No. 1 and No. 2 to land on a sloping shelf. Others should descend a little way into the gap. A long step bridges the break between No. 2 and No. 3, which gives good sport if the crest is followed throughout. No. 4 overhangs above the next gap and is climbed on the right flank by a crack just round the corner or by the face further right. A short rappel is required to reach the little col between the ridge and the final rocks of the mountain; otherwise descend the west flank and walk round. On the east side of the col a steep grassy rake slants down the face and leads to the Upper Shelf near the start of First Pinnacle Chimney (not recommended). A rather unpleasant traverse to the platform below Bell's Groove can also be made from the col. To reach the summit take the broad gully, above. It leads to the west ridge. A gravelly "subterranean" passage at the foot of the gully's left wall also takes one to the west ridge. Such features seem to have intrigued the pioneers of the 1890s but this specimen is now so decayed as to afford more annoyance than amusement.

First ascent: J. Maclay and W. W. Naismith. 1894.

70. WESTERN STONESHOOT   300 feet   Moderate

As the name implies, this gully is filled with rubble, much of it unstable. There is one short pitch, climbed on the left, otherwise the route is a walk.

First ascent: Gilbert Thomson and W. W. Naismith. 1893.

CIR MHOR—CAISTEAL ABHAIL COL SPRINGS

On the slopes west of the col (2046 feet) will be found several springs of water. Traverse horizontally and look for patches of bright green moss which mark the places of issue.

CAISTEAL ABHAIL, 2817 feet

The "Castles", as this peak is popularly known (the literal English translation is "stronghold of the ptarmigan"), consist of a cluster of five buttresses the highest of which is the summit of the mountain. They outcrop on the southern slopes above Coire na h-Uaimh and so get whatever sunshine there is to be had. Two hundred feet below lies another area of exposed rock culminating in a well defined buttress called Portcullis which is situated a short distance to the right of the path going up from the Cir Mhor—Caisteal Abhail Col. The latter is the best means of access from Glen Rosa (via Coire Fionn). Coire na h-Uaimh is the obvious approach from Sannox. The climbs on the lower rocks are dealt with first.

71. PORTCULLIS BUTTRESS 210 feet Very Difficult

The foot of the buttress overhangs and a flanking move from the left is necessary to gain its crest.

(1) 70 feet. Start from the boulder-filled gully on the left of the buttress and scale the wall by a 10 foot crack (grassy). Traverse slab to grass patch and spike belay.

(2) 80 feet. Walk up grass to a corner and climb 8 feet crack on the right; thence to the crest beneath a vertical step.

(3) 40 feet. Move round on to the right wall of the buttress and climb the slab above by an exiguous crack trending leftwards. Then move up to a pile of blocks below a 15 foot overhang.

(4) 20 feet. Tackle overhang direct or climb left wall. Some scrambling and a little wall lead to the top of the buttress.

First ascent: E. J. W. Morrison, H. K. Moneypenny and
    G. C. Curtis. June 1954.

72. LEE CLIMB 175 feet Severe

This route keeps on the left flank of the Portcullis Buttress and starts from the gully about 40 feet above the 10 feet crack beginning the Portcullis route. Enter prominent chimney crack and when it forks take right branch until it is possible to make a leftward traverse to another line of chimneys. Follow these to the top.

First ascent: unknown.

73. AVALANCHE GULLY   200 feet   Very Difficult

This scrappy climb lies immediately right of Portcullis Buttress.

Start under the Portcullis overhang and follow a grass shelf to the right. Go round a corner and ascend straight up to a belay below a steep chimney. Traverse (right) into the gully where there is a pile of "avalanche" debris and go up the gully until it is possible to enter a deeply cut chimney on the right. From the top of this chimney traverse left back into the gully which ends in a through route.

First ascent: G. C. Curtis and Miss G. M. Johnson. September 1945.

74. V GULLY   250 feet   Moderate/Difficult

This route uses the right leg of a well marked V, the only really prominent feature to the right of Portcullis Buttress. The Gully is less unpleasant than most Arran gullies. It gives 200 feet of moderate climbing to a grassy shelf. The final 50 foot pitch on left is difficult in standard but this may be avoided by escaping rightwards.

First ascent: G. H. Townend, H. K. Moneypenny, Miss F. M. King and Miss M. M. Carty. August 1945.

THE CASTLES

75. BUTTRESS 1—THE RIFT   300 feet   Moderate

This route uses a cleft which splits the buttress from top to bottom. About 200 feet of easy climbing over sometimes loose rock leads to a horizontal break. A short pitch follows and then take the right fork which narrows to the final through route exit.

First ascent: E. J. W. Morrison, H. K. Moneypenny and G. C. Curtis. June 1945.

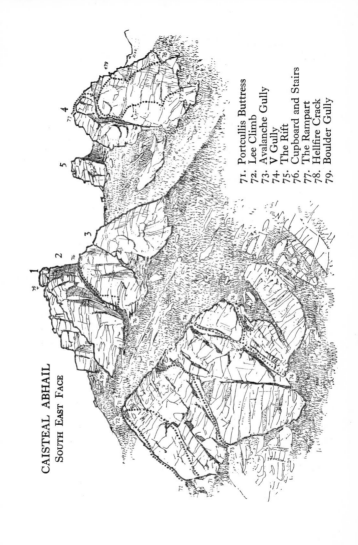

CAISTEAL ABHAIL
SOUTH EAST FACE

71. Portcullis Buttress
72. Lee Climb
73. Avalanche Gully
74. V Gully
75. The Rift
76. Cupboard and Stairs
77. The Rampart
78. Hellfire Crack
79. Boulder Gully

76. BUTTRESS 2—CUPBOARD AND STAIRS   160 feet
Very Difficult

An interesting route which should not be missed.
Start in the gully between 1 and 2 Buttresses about 40 ft.
from the nose of No. 2.

(1) 70 feet. A shelf slopes up from right to left.
Climb up to its left end and thence step up on to a slab
above. Traverse right beneath an overhang containing
a curious pothole (the Cupboard) and so gain the crest
of the buttress.

(2) 50 feet. Ascend the "Stairs" to a 15 foot wall.

(3) 40 feet. Pull up and swing left, finishing either
leftwards or straight up. The top of the buttress is
separated from the parent mountain by a small gap which
is reached by a descent of 10 feet.

First ascent: G. C. Curtis and Miss G. M. Johnson.
September 1945.

Buttress 3. No recorded route.

Buttress 5. The summit tor gives about 100 ft. of scrambling on its west face.

77. BUTTRESS 4—THE RAMPART   455 feet   Difficult

This buttress is the biggest of the group and gives a
fairly interesting if rather scrappy route which follows
the crest with two diversions on the left flank. The foot
of the buttress is a clean cut wall.

(1) 60 feet. Climb the terminal wall 20 feet from its
left edge and go up to a little recess via a slab. Escape up
overhang on the left. *N.B.*—This pitch is VERY DIFFI-
CULT but can be turned on the left.

(2) 40 feet. Go straight up over slabs to little grass
terrace below vertical step.

(3) 40 feet. Surmount vertical step right of centre and

another little wall immediately above. Slabs lead to extensive grass platform.

(4) 100 feet. Almost level promenade to foot of steep wall.

(5) 40 feet. Skirt left corner of wall and traverse into leaning chimney straight ahead. Climb up to second jammed block and take a belay.

(6) 50 feet. Continue up chimney and gain the foot of a large pitted slab. Climb over the slab to a trench stance behind it.

(7) 25 feet. Step up on to sloping shelf on the corner above the trench and pass round to the left flank. Ascend straight up to the crest.

(8) 100 feet. Very pleasant, easy climbing leads to the finish.

First ascent: G. H. Townend, H. K. Moneypenny, Miss
    F. M. King and Miss M. M. Carty. August 1945.

78. BUTTRESS 4—Hellfire Crack   200 feet
Very Difficult

This route lies on the right flank of Buttress 4 and finishes at the pitted slab (Pitch (6)) of the Rampart climb. One of the party on the first ascent apparently burst into flames while struggling in the strenuous chimney, hence the intimidating title.

Begin on the right flank about 100 feet from the foot of the buttress and enter an easy chimney via a little wall. The chimney leads to the large grass terrace. Enter the gully beyond the top right corner of the terrace and from it gain access to a steep V-shaped chimney on the left wall. From the top a rather holdless scoop leads to the right hand end of the "pitted slab". Finish by Rampart.

First ascent: H. K. Moneypenny and G. C. Curtis.
    April 1945.

79. BOULDER GULLY   300 feet   Difficult

This grassy route is really an alternative finish to Hellfire Crack. Instead of taking to the V chimney continue up the gully and cross a steep cleft. Climb the chimney beyond to a recess and escape from this to the right.

First ascent: unknown.

80. CREAG DUBH—15 MINUTE RIDGE   230 feet
Difficult

Creag Dubh lies about 1 mile NNW of Caisteal Abhail and forms the termination of the latter's NW ridge. The crag has several parallel buttresses, the shortest and cleanest of which provides this route. It is situated immediately on the right of the biggest scree gully on the face. Start at the bottom left corner. Traverse rightwards on slabs below overhang and gain the crest by a crack and more slabs. The rest is interesting scrambling on a well defined ridge.

First ascent: Mr and Mrs G. Scott Johnston. September 1945.

CEUM NA CAILLICH, 2300 feet
81. WITCH'S STEP   Moderate

From afar this dramatic cleft appears to separate two fine towers of solid rock but in fact little scope for rock climbing exists. The usual approach is by the eastern ridge of Caisteal Abhail. The descent into the cleft is mainly on loose gravel. From the gap ascend the opposite face by a little diagonal chimney leading to an awkward sloping slab. Above this go straight up to the top and enter a cleft, on the right, splitting the enormous summit block. The rest is obvious. From Glen Sannox make an ascending traverse to the foot of Broomstick Ridge, the narrow band of slabs on the right hand side of the filthy gully leading up to the Step.

82. BROOMSTICK RIDGE 500 feet Moderate or over

This route permits much variation. The line of least resistance is moderate but quite difficult climbing can be had by keeping as close as possible to the left edge. There is a jolly little pinnacle about halfway up.

First ascent: C. E. Willes Johnson (solo.) March 1944.

PART III

OUTLYING CLIMBS

GLENSHANT HILL (1130 feet)

This is the flat-topped "escarpment" on the north side of lower Glen Rosa. Its form is the result of wave action when at one time the land was 1000 ft. lower than it is now. There is a curious split pinnacle just below the lip and further right (i.e. east) a line of little cliffs composed of schist (unaltered). The pinnacle is best seen from a little beyond the bridge over the Garbh Allt going *down* the glen. It is about 18 feet high on the inner side and 40 feet on the outer. There are several routes to be had but hardly of sufficient interest to justify the tedious approach slog. Similar remarks apply to the line of cliffs where a number of short routes exist.

MAOL DONN (1208 feet)

About 2 miles south of Corrie Hotel and dominating the coastal road is a square-topped bluff with a belt of sandstone cliffs on its north face. The principal route lies up a deeply cut 100 feet chimney, difficult in standard.

83. STACACH BUTTRESS (COIRE LAN)   350 feet
Difficult

At the head of the corrie drained by the White Water burn, which enters the sea near Corrie, several little buttresses descend from the tors on the ridge connecting Goat Fell and North Goat Fell. A route has been made up the last but one nearest Goat Fell. There is scope for variation and opportunities to escape.

First ascent: E. W. Rudge and party.

THE CORRIE BOULDERS

These four famous erratic blocks may give some evening amusement to climbers staying at Corrie or Sannox but otherwise are not worth a special visit. Their location is as follows:

CLACH MHOR (the largest, said to weigh 620 tons). 100 yards from the road a short distance south of the White Water.

CLACH AN FHIONN (Hero's Stone). 400 yards north of the Schoolhouse between the road and the sea.

CLACH A' CHAIT (Cat Stone). ¾ mile out of Corrie on the Sannox road (left side, going north). Much superior to the others in technical interest.

ROCKING STONE. On the right-hand side of the road just before one reaches the first house in the village of Sannox. There is a commodious cave on the other side of the road, which is worth exploring.

TORR NEAD AN EOIN (1057 feet)

This hill lies 1½ miles SE of Lochranza. There is a geologically interesting rock face on its west side for the northern part is of schist and the southern of granite. The granite is too broken up to yield a good route but the steep northern buttress gives a reasonable climb of 250 feet approx. Start near the centre and go up to an open groove which leads to a grass ledge. From the ledge there is a choice of route. Continue up the groove (Severe) or traverse left until a line of weakness gives access to the slabs higher up (Very Difficult). A vegetatious gully bounds the schist buttress on the right. It has four pitches (Difficult) and has been appropriately named Verdant Gully.

CREAG NA H-IOLAIRE (Eagle's Crag) 1379 feet

This impressive cliff lies on the eastern slopes of Glen Catacol, about 1½ miles from the sea. No actual routes have been recorded but it might repay a visit if one happened to be in its vicinity.

N.W. RIDGE OF BEINN BHARRAIN

The western hills of Arran are composed of a fine crystalled granite which has withstood the weathering of time much less successfully than its coarse neighbour. As a result, whatever cliffs existed at one time have now been reduced to rubble. Anyone moved to ascend the highest summit of the group should choose the North-West Ridge which lies 1½ miles east of Pirnmill. It is well defined and gives some scrambling. The ridge terminates on the north top (the higher) of the mountain.

DRUMADOON PINNACLE

Near Blackwaterfoot there are some cliffs and a detached pinnacle, 20 feet high on its inner side and 60 feet on its outer. It gives a jolly little climb and similar amusement may be had on the nearby cliffs.

HOLY ISLAND

The western slope of this charming island is tiered with small cliffs of porphyry and claystone which yield some incidental sport to those wise enough to visit the place. The standard approach is by swimming across the channel from Kingscross Point (Severe for moderate swimmers).

CLASSIFIED LIST OF CLIMBS

VERY SEVERE

HARD SEVERE

SEVERE

MILD SEVERE

VERY DIFFICULT

DIFFICULT

MODERATE

EASY

APPENDIX OF NEW CLIMBS

The following routes are not shown on the diagrams in the main text but, where possible, their approximate locations are given by such references as 24/25. This means that the route following lies somewhere between routes 24 and 25 of the main Guide. In some cases it has not been possible to use this convention.

A'CHIR

24/25. HANGOVER SLAB   630 feet   Mild Severe

A rather artificial but enjoyable climb between Gullies 5 and 6. Starts some 60 feet left of Gully 6.

(1) 140 feet. Climb clean slab, over detached block and slight bulge, to vegetatious corner. Climb this, or slab on right and trend left to block belay below overhang.

(2) 150 feet. Through this overhang, then up slabs to piton belay.

(3) 60 feet. Up slabs to heather terrace.

(4) 80 feet. Pull up through overhang, then up slabs.

(5) 80 feet. Up slabs to heather ledge; piton belay.

(6) 120 feet. Up short severe wall, then traverse right to turn overhang and up easy slabs to large blocks.

First ascent: J. Stewart and A. Cowmeadow (both E.U.M.C.). May 1961.

27/28. AFTERTHOUGHT   290 feet   Severe

(1) 40 feet. Climb slabs immediately left of Giant's Staircase to grass ledge.

(2) 120 feet. Climb wall by cracks and mantelshelf on to detached flake; a very good pitch. Up by cracks to a block, traverse right round bulge and layback to heather ledge and flake belay.

(3) 130 feet. Up over flake to overhang, then traverse right and up to blocks. Trend right to block below cave and reach ridge through cave.

First ascent: A. Cowmeadow and J. Stewart. May 1961.

29/30. NOVEMBER CHIMNEY	180 feet
	Very Difficult

From the "little col" mentioned in the description of route 19, page 28, descend the gully on the Iorsa or west side to a 60 feet wall on the south margin of the gully. The only breach in the wall is a prominent curving chimney topped by a large chockstone.

(1) 60 feet. Climb this narrow and strenuous chimney: the chock is firm and there is a good belay 15 feet beyond it (crux).

(2) 90 feet. Move right to easier rocks leading to foot of slabs, which are gained by a variety of cracks. Belay about half way up slabs.

(3) 30 feet. Continue up slabs to crest of ridge.

First ascent: J. W. Simpson and W. Wallace. November 1958.

CIR MHOR: ROSA FACE

35/36. FOURTH WALL—HOCKEY VARIATION	
105 feet	Severe

(1) to (7) Follow route 35.

(8a) 55 feet. From grass patch at base of plinth traverse 15 feet right and descend to sloping grass corner. Make delicate, exposed upward traverse to right across slab, until possible to ascend directly.

(9a) 50 feet. Climb broken slab above until barred by overhanging roof and reach crest of ridge by a spectacular exit to right.

First ascent: R. A. Hockey. September 1959.

35/41. ROSA PINNACLE GIRDLE   1,000 feet
Very Severe

(1) (2) and (3) 160 feet. As for route 35.

(4) 60 feet. Up groove for 20 feet, then up right to line of knobbles leading to belay in Sou'Wester Slabs (below flake cracks).

(5) 40 feet. Obvious traverse from below belay round corner to a belay in Sickle.

(6) 70 feet. Up and right to exposed corner. Traverse steep wall (avoiding loose flake) into the Layback Crack of the South Ridge; descend this to belay.

(7) (8)and (9) 145 feet. Reverse South Ridge to foot of the Y Crack.

(10) 60 feet. Follow easy terrace to Original Route, go down this 15 feet to grass patch, then make descending traverse on right wall to a rib; climb this to niche and flake belay.

(11) 30 feet. Hand traverse under overhang to grass tuft. Continue, up then down round corner to belay.

(12) 100 feet. Down round corner then up right to mantelshelf. Follow dwindling ledge into bottomless layback corner. Climb this for 15 feet, leave on right and traverse into Lower East Chimney.

(13) 100 feet. Climb cracked slab on right to flake and traverse right above overhang into groove (piton runner). Cross rib into another groove and climb to pinnacle belay.

(14) 120 feet. Climb crack above and traverse easily right to jammed block.

(15) 100 feet. Continue into Sub Rosa Gully.

The traverse could be prolonged by using Minotaur and upper Labyrinth.

First ascent: R. Campbell and N. McNiven (both E.U.M.C.). May 1961.

36.5/37. HAMMER   245 feet   Very Severe

Starts at a cairn below a crack about 90 feet *downhill* from Route 35: not to be confused with the start of Anvil which is several feet to right and has a broader crack.

(1) 25 feet. Climb prominent crack to belay.

(2) 120 feet. Move left on to steep slab above a deep crack still further left. Climb edge, fixing runner round chock-stone. Go a little right and climb steep grassy crack without positive holds to large ledge.

(3) 100 feet. Follow a crack in the same general line for 40 feet, then traverse diagonally right using a line of "dimples" to reach the foot of the Layback Crack of the South Ridge Direct Route.

First ascent: D. Sim and D. Cameron (Greenock M.C.). August 1960.

36.5/37. ANVIL   180 feet   Very Severe

(1) 25 feet. Climb broad crack (a few feet right of Hammer) to stance left of small overhang.

(2) 70 feet. Using piton descend 10 feet and tension traverse right to gain holds leading through overhang to sloping platform. If done "free" this section is exceptionally delicate. A thin crack now leads to grass ledges and a belay on the right.

(3) 60 feet. Continue leftwards by grooves to small cave and belay.

(4) 25 feet. Break out by right wall, awkwardly, to reach easy slab leading to crest of South Ridge (top of Pitch 4 Direct Route).

First ascent: D. McKelvie and R. Richardson (both Greenock M.C.). August 1960.

GOAT FELL: ROSA SLABS

ANGELS' PAVEMENT   270 feet   Mild Severe

Starts at highest point of grassy rake which passes above the first slab of Evening Traverse; reached by heather slopes left of the watercourse.

(1) 70 feet. Climb the slab to rightmost of two cracks splitting overlap of upper slab; climb bulge to flake belay.

(2) 60 feet. Climb to chain of pitted holds in the slab above and follow it to indefinite ledge and poor flake belay.

(3) 30 feet. Traverse easily left to small belay.

(4) 110 feet. Straight up slab over two small overlaps (the second being left of a grass clump) to a terrace. Continue by Fools' Causeway.

First ascent: G. Kilgour and N. McNiven. July 1960.

FOOLS' CAUSEWAY   300 feet   Very Severe

From finish of Angels' Pavement traverse left over broken ground to a smooth water-streaked slab, above its lowest waterslide section and at the point where two blocks form a thread belay.

(1) 80 feet. Gain foot of slab from the left; a few feet higher follow a very thin grassy crack slanting rightwards. From its end go up a few feet and take piton belay in rock pocket.

(2) 120 feet. Climb up rightwards using friction to a line of pocket holds leading to a tiny groove; this becomes a layback crack curving left to a small overhang. Above this an easier groove and slab lead to a ledge.

(3) 100 feet. Finish by easier slabs to Second Terrace near its upper end.

First ascent: G. Kilgour and N. McNiven. July 1960.

SOUTH SLABS, I   300 feet   Severe

At the base of the slab area some 400 yards to the south of Rosa Slabs a fault will be noticed running up to the left. This feature marks the start of the route.

(1) 190 feet. Climb easily up the fault as far as it goes.

(2) 110 feet. Take line of least resistance up slabs to easy ground and a belay.

First ascent: D. McKelvie and D. Sim. July 1958.

SOUTH SLABS, II   280 feet   Hard Severe

Start at bottom right hand corner of the slabs (cairn).

(1) 70 feet. Up moderate slabs and grooves, slanting left to grassy hollow, providing a stance.

(2) 100 feet. Go up grass and steep slabs to narrow grass band below small overlap. Climb to stance and belay.

(3) 30 feet. Up 15 feet, then left to stance on small ledge; piton belay.

(4) 80 feet. Move up diagonally left on friction holds to foot of thin crack in corner (fix piton runner); then up line of cracks to nook on left; stance. The difficulties are sustained in this pitch and it was done in socks on the first ascent.

(5) 30 feet. Easy scrambling to finish.

First ascent: W. Wallace and D. McCulloch (J.M.C.S.). September 1961.

CIOCH NA H-OIGHE

53/54. THE BASTION—TIDEMARK   360 feet
Hard Severe

This exposed climb follows an obvious gangway, which runs round the upper part of the Bastion (see route 53), and starts at a good spike belay just above Ledge 3, some 200 feet from its upper end.

(1) 100 feet. From belay cross two slabs to large block.

(2) 70 feet. The gangway is now seen at the end of a grass ledge. Cross to good belay a few feet up the gangway.

(3) 90 feet. Follow gangway to its finish in an overhanging wall; belay.

(4) 100 feet. Descend 10 feet, then traverse across and up slabs to Ledge 4; block belay.

First ascent: A. Maxfield and J. Peacock. June 1960.

CIR MHOR: SANNOX FACE

—/57. GREENFINGER GROOVES   500 feet
Very Severe

The base of the Lower N.E. Face is undercut by a prominent overhang. The route starts some 70 feet from the right hand end of the overhang and left of it, at a groove just left of and 30 feet below a small black hanging corner.

(1) 80 feet. Move over the undercut base and up a thin groove, turning the bulge by a crack leading right to a spike near the black corner. Go left and continue up the groove to its finish 15 feet beneath an overhang. Piton belay.

(2) 40 feet. Step up then down again to the right and very delicately across the slab to reach a good grass ledge. Piton belay.

(3) 100 feet. The hanging corner on the left is ascended to the bulge, which is turned on the left (crux) to a spike runner above. Continue up grooves to a small stance and piton belay.

(4) 150 feet. Grassy grooves lead to a long grassy ledge. Go right, along this to the base of a wet groove; piton belay.

(5) 130 feet. Up the groove to good block belay in the bed of Gully A. Descend easily to the corrie or continue upwards using April Arete. (q.v.)

First ascent: R. Brown (Manchester Gritstone C.C.) and T. Howard. August 1961.

In the 1962 S.M.C. Journal there is a sketchy account of a climb called Nor'easter Slabs, done in May 1961 by N. McNiven and R. Campbell, which seems to follow the same line as Greenfinger Grooves. The start is marked by a cairn of orange peel!

—/57. APRIL ARETE   450 feet   Severe

This route goes up the narrow edge formed by the left wall of Gully A.

(1) 150 feet. Follow the left rib of the Gully, making occasional moves on to the vertical wall where necessary, to a block belay.

(2) 100 feet. An awkward little wall, then on up the edge to a belay level with the huge chockstone in the Gully.

(3) 50 feet. Move up and out on to the Gully wall and reach the grassy top of the chockstone along small ledges. Belay down back.

(4) 150 feet. Left on to the rib again, which leads back into the Gully and thence by scrambling to the top.

First ascent: J. W. Simpson and W. Wallace. April 1959.

—/57. EASTERN RIDGE   300 feet   Difficult

At the top of Gully A there is a vertical wall. This route starts in a crack beginning at its left edge.

(1) 100 feet. Up crack curving right past jammed blocks to pleasant slabs and a good ledge with a belay.

(2) and (3) 200 feet. Further cracks and slabs wander pleasantly up the ridge, keeping near the right edge all the way.

First ascent: R. Brown and T. Howard August 1961.

The combination of Greenfinger Grooves, April Arete and Eastern Ridge gives 1,250 feet of almost continuous climbing as was first done by Messrs Brown and Howard, who gave the name XANADU to it.

59/60. B2-C RIB VARIATION   100 feet approx.
                                                    Severe

About half way up the Rib a spacious grassy ledge is reached. Instead of following original directly up, traverse right after a few feet to the edge overlooking Gully C; ascend this edge to the top of the Rib in one run out.

First ascent: Miss G. W. Hamilton and W. Wallace. Easter 1959.

GLEN SANNOX: COIRE NA H-UAIMH

SLAPSTICK WALL   375 feet   Severe

On the right hand side of the belt of slabs forming the lip of Coire na h'Uaimh, there is an overlap shaped like the letter J, which marks the general line of this route.

(1) 40 feet. Start 300 feet right of lowest rocks (cairn and arrow) to left of steep east facing little slab. Climb into upper of two corners and continue for 25 feet until exit can be made to slab on right and then on to ledges.

(2) 50 feet. Follow easy grassy cracks to piton belay.

(3) 70 feet. Keep in crack above until exit made by mantelshelf move to right.

(4) 105 feet. Traverse 10 feet right and descend to slab. Continue by corner for 40 feet until original line can be regained; take piton belay above awkward lay-back section.

(5) 110 feet. Up and left on to slab until spike belay is reached.

First ascent: R. Hutchison Jr., J. Gardner and W. Gartshore (all Lomond M.C.). September 1959.

OUTLYING CLIMBS

BEINN BHARRAIN: NORTH RIDGE

The following routes lie on the craggy east side of a ridge coming from the north on to Beinn Bharrain; the map reference of the crag is 898429. In the middle of the face there is a buttress with a conspicuous crack running from bottom right to top left.

ROUTE I   200 feet   Severe

(1) 100 feet. Climb crack to belay at the top.

(2) 100 feet. Traverse left for 20 feet, then up 10-foot wall. Easier climbing leads to the top.

First ascent: A. Maxfield and J. Peacock. June 1960.

ROUTE II   200 feet   Hard Severe

Start at right angled corner 40 feet left of Route I.

(1) 100 feet. Climb crack in corner till a difficult move to the left gives access to slabs above. Follow slabs to belay.

(2) 40 feet. Traverse easily leftwards until below upper part of crag.

(3) 60 feet. Go up the middle of an undulating wall to reach the finish.

First ascent: A. Maxfield and J. Peacock. June 1960.